TWO EQUALS ONE

A MARRIAGE EQUATION FOR LOVE, LAUGHTER & LONGEVITY

JIMMY ROLLINS & IRENE ROLLINS

W PUBLISHING GROUP

AN IMPRINT OF THOMAS NELSON

Published in Nashville, Tennessee, by W Publishing, an imprint of Thomas Nelson.

Published in association with The Bindery Agency, www.thebinderyagency.com. Contributing Editor: Heather Preston

Thomas Nelson titles may be purchased in bulk for educational, business, fundraising, or sales promotional use. For information, please email SpecialMarkets@ThomasNelson.com. Any internet addresses, phone numbers, or company or product information printed in this book are offered as a resource and are not intended in any way to be or to imply an endorsement by Thomas Nelson, nor does Thomas Nelson vouch for the existence, content, or services of these sites, phone numbers, companies, or products beyond the life of this book.

Unless otherwise noted, Scripture quotations are taken from the Holy Bible, New International Version®, NIV®. Copyright © 1973, 1978, 1984, 2011 by Biblica, Inc.® Used by permission of Zondervan. All rights reserved worldwide. www.zondervan.com. The "NIV" and "New International Version" are trademarks registered in the United States Patent and Trademark Office by Biblica, Inc.®

Scripture quotations marked AMP are taken from the Amplified® Bible (AMP). Copyright © 2015 by The Lockman Foundation. Used by permission. www.Lockman.org

Scripture quotations marked ESV are taken from the ESV® Bible (The Holy Bible, English Standard Version®). Copyright © 2001 by Crossway, a publishing ministry of Good News Publishers. Used by permission. All rights reserved.

Scripture quotations marked KJV are taken from the King James Version. Public domain.

Scripture quotations marked MSG are taken from THE MESSAGE. Copyright © 1993, 2002, 2018 by Eugene H. Peterson. Used by permission of NavPress. All rights reserved. Represented by Tyndale House Publishers, a Division of Tyndale House Ministries.

Scripture quotations marked NKJV are taken from the New King James Version®. Copyright © 1982 by Thomas Nelson. Used by permission. All rights reserved.

Scripture quotations marked NLT are taken from the Holy Bible, New Living Translation. Copyright © 1996, 2004, 2015 by Tyndale House Foundation. Used by permission of Tyndale House Ministries, Carol Stream, Illinois 60188. All rights reserved.

Scripture quotations marked THE VOICE are taken from The Voice™. Copyright © 2012 by Ecclesia Bible Society. Used by permission. All rights reserved.

Names and identifying characteristics of some individuals have been changed to preserve their privacy.

This book provides general guidance and support for marriage and relationships. It is not intended to replace professional counseling or therapy. Always seek the advice of a qualified professional with any questions you may have regarding your specific situation. The authors and publisher assume no responsibility for any injuries, damages, or losses incurred as a result of the use or application of the information contained herein.

ISBN 978-0-7852-9006-3 (audiobook)
ISBN 978-0-7852-9005-6 (ePub)
ISBN 978-0-7852-8983-8 (softcover)

Library of Congress Control Number: 2024937289

Printed in the United States of America

24 25 26 27 28 LBC 5 4 3 2 1

To our precious children, Kayla, Jaden, and Maya.

We are forever grateful God gave us the gift of each of you to go on this journey of life with. Thank you for forgiving our mistakes as parents when we were sick and at our worst. Thank you for your grace, love, and forgiveness as we worked through the messy growth times in our marriage. Our hope for you is that you would also pursue purpose from the pain we have gone through as a family. God did his part and we had to do ours, and you courageously joined us on our journey from dysfunction to our God purpose. We pray that our roadblocks become your hurdles and that you give away all you got through our miracle journey and inspire those around you with the light of Jesus. The power of reconciliation rests on you, too, just as it does on the both of us. The three of you are going to change generations because of leaning into growing with us. Our prayer is that we have modeled rupture and repair in marriage and demonstrated that we *do hard things*! We pray that you continually pursue God and emotional health and choose spouses who are willing to do the work to be emotionally healthy. *Two* equally crazy people who are equally committed to doing the work can have a marriage made *one*.

Rollins 5 for life!

LOVE,

MOM & DAD

CONTENTS

FOREWORD

When you encounter a couple who is fun and easy to be around, there is usually a depth and a story behind the sweetness. Jimmy and Irene are a couple who leave a trail of laughter behind them, and the way they interact and approach their relationship is refreshing and kind and tender. The way they got there is a road marked by pain, heartache, and struggle, but with it, so much redemption, joy, hard work, and grace.

We remember sitting across from them at a dinner table, after Irene had preached about her story in our church. Getting to listen to what God had done in their lives was astonishing and wonderful. Their vulnerability has changed everything for them in their relationship and has increased intimacy in every way.

If you are looking for encouragement and a challenge in your relationship, if you are wanting greater depth in your marriage, the Rollins are the couple for the job.

The more we hear from them and learn from them, the more we can learn to see each other with deeper understanding and empathy. Their book *Two Equals One* is Jimmy and Irene's guide to seeing your spouse as your teammate and partner and seeing that your relationship has the potential to be fun, deep, and enjoyable.

They have worked through hard days to see the beauty of God's work in them and through them, and you are wise to lean into their wisdom and to glean the truth they have lived out in their lives and in their marriage. Hang on tight, get ready for an incredible ride, and be ready to learn and grow into the arms of our good and loving God and into the arms of your spouse. It's going to be good, and you better believe you will laugh your way through.

LEVI AND JENNIE LUSKO, BESTSELLING AUTHORS OF
THE MARRIAGE DEVOTIONAL, FOUNDERS OF FRESH LIFE
CHURCH, AND PODCAST HOSTS OF *HEY! IT'S THE LUSKOS*

INTRODUCTION

LET'S GET REAL

Are you ready for real talk? Are you tired of marriage books filled with endless lists of dos and don'ts or cliché pep talks? Do you crave intimacy with your spouse, but you've started to feel a strain?

Are you frustrated because you and your spouse lack the tools to communicate effectively? Are you worn out from all the ups and downs? Has your marriage started to feel hard, and you wish you had a reset button?

Maybe you've been asking yourself whether you have what it takes to make this relationship work. Is it even worth it? Do you even like this person anymore?

We've been there! And if you're ready to get personal—with some raw, authentic, firsthand talk about marriage—this book is for you.

LEARNING THE HARD WAY

We are two equally crazy, equally committed people who are more in love today than we were in those whirlwind-romance days of our dating years. But learning how to thrive in our marriage definitely hasn't been an easy process. As of the writing of this book, we've been married for more than twenty-five years and we've navigated many difficulties, including food and alcohol addictions, family dysfunction, and communication issues as well as other challenging and painful seasons.

For the first fifteen years of our marriage, we did our best to manage the challenges of family life while navigating the complexities of our professional life as pastors of a thriving church. We knew how to project the image of a happy, healthy marriage, but it was only an illusion. Behind the smiles our marriage was on the verge of divorce, and we had grown so far apart that not only were we unable to meet each other's needs, but we weren't even aware of our own needs.

This balancing act came to a screeching halt when the demands of our public professional ministry life and private family and marriage life became too much for two broken individuals, from two very different backgrounds, to manage. It was time for us to get help and pursue the healing we desperately needed and longed for.

If you want to know how we found our way back to love—and if you also want to find your way back to love—this book is your guide to becoming healthy and whole as you learn how to rebuild and strengthen your marriage. As we tackle the tough topics, we won't shy away from the nitty-gritty details; we'll be vulnerable about our own failures and weaknesses because we've found freedom on the other side, and we want you to experience that same freedom with your spouse.

We wrote this book because we want you to know freedom from your past, from your present hang-ups, and from the feeling of hopelessness that plagues—and all too often ends—so many marriages today. Through our Two Equals One marriage and coaching ministry, we've helped thousands of married couples deal with past and present issues to develop a two-equals-one marriage, and we pray that you, too, will find healing in these pages. You'll have to take risks and put in some work, but if you're ready to enjoy the fulfillment of a healthy marriage, keep reading!

WHAT IS TWO EQUALS ONE?

Throughout this journey, we will be referring to our formula for marriage: two equals one. Just to be clear, two equals one isn't an invitation to codependency. It's not a comfortable marriage; it's passionate. It's not figuring out how to compromise; it's figuring out how to complement.

For years we lived the way many married people do—with each other but not for each other. Two equals two—and although a husband and wife may love each other, each one is ultimately in it for his or her own dreams and desires. This was our story until we realized God's Word gives us a different equation.

Two equals one is not a formula we invented. It's not the kind of formula mainstream culture gives—society's formulas are constantly changing and, frankly, don't work. Two equals one is actually one of the first gifts that God gave us in his Word.

We'll explain more in this book, but this formula for a fulfilling marriage hasn't changed for thousands of years, and it still works today. It's not easy, and it will require you and your spouse to work together, but two really can equal one.

LOVE, LAUGHTER, AND LONGEVITY

There are so many things we'll cover—it may seem overwhelming. But, in the end, it's simple. Everything we will discuss in this book comes down to three essential tools for a thriving marriage: love, laughter, and longevity.

Part 1 is all about *love*. Society has plenty to say about what love is, and mostly its ideas fail. So we're going to talk about how the Bible defines love—its real definition. We'll show you how your expectations and preconceived ideas about love can hinder you from staying in love.

Part 2 is all about *laughter*. It might sound trivial, but there's a reason that couples who laugh together stay together—and it's not simply because they're having fun. Couples who laugh together have learned how to communicate. Without communication and understanding, a two-equals-one marriage is impossible.

Finally, in part 3 we'll talk about *longevity*. This is where we put into practice all we've learned to make a two-equals-one marriage last. This isn't a sprint, it's a marathon. And if you've ever witnessed a runner finish a marathon, you've watched a calculated athlete. Someone in mastery of his or her body, who doesn't take the sport of running lightly but trains intentionally to last all twenty-six miles. Your marriage can go the distance, but only if you're willing to put in the work.

- Maybe your marriage is on the brink of failure, and this book is a last resort. We've been there. We'll show you the tools we used not only to save our marriage but to find each other.
- Maybe your marriage is losing what culture describes as "magic," and you're getting more frustrated than excited to be around each other. This book is for you. We'll help you identify and address the root issues before the symptoms get too serious.
- Maybe you're not married yet but you're headed toward that commitment—again, this book is for you! Let the lessons we learned the hard way spare you from the same.

- If your marriage is stronger than ever, that's fantastic—but this book is *still* for you because the best time to get help is before you need it.

Our goal is for this book to be like your personal trainer; your best days can be ahead of you, but you're responsible for the work. In each chapter we will be transparent in our story, sharing from our individual perspectives and then coming together as one.

There will be times while reading this book that you will want to take a moment and breathe. Although you might be tempted to skip over some sections, we promise they're all worth your time. So don't rush through or skip to the end—breathe.

Each chapter concludes with a prayer and a practical challenge, and we highly recommend doing these. We have found that practice makes permanent—you become what you repeatedly do. In part 1 the challenges are individual. In parts 2 and 3 the challenges are designed for you to do with your spouse.

Your story is not over! Wherever your marriage is currently, we want to help you get back to a place of love, laughter, and longevity. A place where *two equals one*.

PART ONE

LOVE

What caused you to fall in love with your spouse?

Love is an elusive concept. You may be hard-pressed to name one single thing that caused you to fall in love with the person you married. Even more challenging, many of us don't fall in love with someone who is exactly like us or even very similar—we may be drawn to someone quite different. And while in the initial phases of a relationship differences can be exciting, eventually those differences can lead to friction . . . and not the kind that causes a good spark.

Today's culture equates love with a feeling—that feeling we get slow dancing or the dramatic rush of feelings we get watching a romantic movie. Sometimes we define love by what we've seen or previously experienced, maybe even substitute love with lust. The problem is that all of these definitions last for only a moment, not long beyond the words "I do."

So how do you make a marriage work?

We almost didn't. By appearances, we could've fooled you! We looked every bit the part: both pastors of a thriving church, with three beautiful children, living in a nice house in a great neighborhood—and yet our marriage almost didn't survive.

This part is all about love because we believe that if we take a hard look at how we define *love* and what exactly love means to us, we can better understand ourselves and our spouses. We can better understand why the things that attracted us initially now cause conflict, or what our expectations were when we said "I do" versus what they are now.

We'll talk about where these expectations of love come from. Now, a lot of this will get personal because these are lessons we learned the hard way. You'll hear from us individually, each telling our version of events, and then we'll share from the lens of having worked through it together. We want to give you the tools we didn't have.

Hopefully, by learning from our painful experiences and hard-fought battles, you won't have to endure what we did. But if you're in the middle of the kind of crisis in which we found ourselves, please know that you're not alone. More importantly, there is hope and healing as you discover the tools for a marriage made whole.

Yes, you can take two very different people with two very different backgrounds and have a happy, thriving marriage! *Two really can equal one.*

CHAPTER ONE

GOD'S EQUATION FOR MARRIAGE

Two equals one isn't something we
came up with—it's God's equation!

Did you have to do household chores growing up? Which one was your least favorite?

I (Jimmy) hated sweeping the floors using a dustpan. You collect all that nastiness—food crumbs, lint, dirt people tracked in on their shoes—into a pile. Then you have to collect said pile onto the dustpan so you can transfer it into the trash. The trouble is that this task not only takes time but also is just generally a terrible chore.

What's much easier, though, is to simply lift the corner of a nearby rug and sweep the dirt under it. Out of sight, out of mind, right?

As terrible as this method of dealing with dirt sounds (I do not recommend it, especially because I got caught when I tried this as a child), it is often what we do with our issues at home. We sweep them under the rug, so to speak. It's what Irene and I did for years.

But the truth is, all that dirt is still there, and in marriage you can avoid conflict for only so long. Eventually it comes to the surface. Irritation leads to confusion, which creates frustration—and before long everything becomes an argument. What starts as small disagreements, if left unresolved, can become full-blown resentments.

REAL TALK

Irene

"I want a divorce."

The sting of those words as Jimmy slammed the bedroom door behind him was like an open-handed slap. *How can he say that to me? After all we've been through?*

As those four words reverberated in my ears, I felt my face flush red— and I really needed a drink. In my substance-controlled mind, Jimmy was the most selfish person I had ever met. He was the problem, not me.

Instead of having an open dialogue, however, I decided to snoop. Jimmy had left his phone unattended, and I'm not really sure what I thought I would find, but as I scrolled through his text messages alone in an empty corner of our house, I began to panic. He had been collecting evidence, texting with friends and family members, including sharing pictures, documenting my problem with alcohol. I suddenly realized his ultimatum of divorce was no idle threat, and he could blow up everything we had worked so hard for.

I sank to the floor, head in my hands, and fumed. *Why couldn't he just cover for me? Isn't that what a loving spouse should do? How dare he turn on me like this!*

In hindsight I know that these internal questions were the thoughts of an addict. But I had grown up with the understanding that what happened in the family stayed in the family, so Jimmy's sharing of our personal issues felt like a violation of my privacy. I felt exposed, and the feeling of being on trial made me defensive.

I couldn't see that he had run out of options. I couldn't see that he was trying to save our family. And I couldn't see beyond my own anger and shame, both of which were keeping me from even admitting I had a problem.[1]

Later that evening I confronted him with the text messages. His gaze was unwavering, but there were tears brimming in his eyes. I stood there, hand on my hip, holding his phone in anticipation. But instead of offering me the apology I had expected from him, he replied, "You need to get help with your drinking." His voice quivered a bit, the pain almost tangible, as he continued, "Or I'm going to leave."

My jaw fell. My initial rage turned to confusion, then shame. The idea of losing my marriage, my children, my reputation, my ministry, and the church Jimmy and I had labored so long to build was overwhelming. Nervously spinning the ring on my left hand, a ring that now felt like a symbol of betrayal, I felt cornered.

Threats of splitting had been flung at each other before, in the heat of an argument, but this time it was different—and that realization had me reeling. The spiral in my mind made me want to drink. Although the evidence on my husband's phone and his ultimatum were clear, my vision of reality was obscured. It was as if I were seeing my life through the bottom of a glass—everything was distorted.

How did we get here?

My husband of fifteen years wanted a divorce, and from where I stood, it seemed entirely my fault.

Jimmy

Anyone who knows me will attest that I am not a man who is ever at a loss for words. But that day Irene had me speechless. That ultimatum was my last resort, and it was the most difficult thing I have ever done.

As much as I knew I loved Irene, we weren't happy, and we hadn't been for a long time. But we had done a phenomenal job keeping up appearances. Now, this wasn't a conscious maneuver—we weren't trying to be manipulative or fake. There were glimpses of the love we felt in the beginning all along the way. Sometimes I felt as though I were going crazy—as though somehow I was doing marriage wrong but I couldn't figure out how to get it right.

Though keeping up appearances wasn't a conscious effort, we had managed to convince everyone that we had a Hallmark-worthy marriage, and we had faked it for long enough it was like being on autopilot. We'd often get requests to speak at marriage conferences! We'd show up, pose for all the right pictures under the ring lights for social media photo ops, and say all the right things onstage, but as soon as we walked offstage, our smiles would fade and the pain of emptiness would be right back.

We had no business being behind a microphone; we should have been taking notes at those marriage conferences. But I was addicted to ministry—it seemed the one area in my life where I was validated. I knew that to keep moving forward and to be successful, we had to pretend everything was okay. We had to look like the goal line, like the trophy won at the end of a successful united effort. The problem is that when you focus everything on offense, you leave your family vulnerable and unprotected.

One evening I was at pastors' event, surrounded by my peers— guys I wanted in my corner, whose approval meant a lot. We had all been invited to the Duke versus University of North Carolina basketball game. If you follow college basketball, you know that's a prime-time game! Our seats were incredible, but I was so overweight at the time as a result of my food addiction that I couldn't fit in the standard stadium chair. I remember awkwardly angling my body and trying to hide my embarrassment.

That's when I got a text from my youngest daughter that read, "Mom is sleeping in the bathroom." My heart sank. I knew what had happened. I stalled a bit, asking her to text a picture, but I knew the scenario: Irene had had a few too many drinks and passed out. I cautiously glanced around as the photo in my messages confirmed my suspicion.

I had a choice to make. I knew that if I left the game early, everyone would ask why. So to save face in front of all the other pastors, I told my daughter that her mom was simply taking a nap, and I stayed at the game.

Think about that. There was a glaringly obvious problem in our home; my wife and my daughter were crying out for help, but I couldn't see it—I didn't want to. There were no time-outs in ministry. But concealing our secrets and addictions was killing us. I think back on the faces of those men whose approval meant so much to me. One is no longer married; two are no longer in ministry. One committed suicide. I can't help but ask myself whether our lives would look different today if we had been willing to be vulnerable, transparent. To confess rather than conceal our issues.

If you had shown up to our church on Sunday, you would've seen what we wanted people to see: a happy, functional family. But the truth is, "pulpit Jimmy" wasn't the same as "at-home Jimmy." Preaching was everything for me—I knew from a young age I had a gift, but to keep doing it I was convinced that Irene and I had to maintain our image, and that meant hiding anything that wasn't perfect or polished.

The moment I gave Irene the ultimatum, I saw myself as the hero of our family. I saw her as the one with the problem—I was the one holding it all together, holding our family together. But in reality I was just as broken as she was. Instead of showing up for my wife and helping her heal, I would simply cope with my own pain. Whenever ministry wasn't filling the void, I turned to food. I started eating away my feelings and put on an unhealthy amount of weight. Sometimes food wasn't enough, so I turned to pornography. My escapism obliterated the last hope Irene and I had of intimacy.

Neither of us was healthy.

Neither of us knew how to help the other.

I made my living through communication, but I had no idea how to talk to Irene about what was going on. We were on a fast track to ending our marriage. Without words to express or even imagine an alternative, I told my bride I wanted a divorce.

GOD'S EQUATION FOR MARRIAGE

This is much more than a "how to avoid divorce" book. You may or may not resonate with our struggles, but if you don't, it's probably because you're all too aware that you need to be putting in the work to have a healthy marriage. The lessons we learned are good news because our marriage is proof that not only can God redeem any situation, but he can restore and use the brokenness too. Nothing is wasted in his hands.

It's difficult to express how far we've come since that evening. When we preach at marriage conferences now, our relationship is stronger off the stage than when we're speaking on it. There is a tremendous gap between where we were then and where we are now. This is the story of how our whole world changed and the lessons we learned along the way.

For us, it all started with three simple words: *two equals one.*

Understanding that simple phrase changed everything. For the first fifteen years of our marriage, we didn't understand that equation. We lived *with* each other but not *for* each other. We accommodated one another's differences but never fully embraced them.

This was our story until we realized God's Word gives us a different equation. It's one of

Not only can God redeem any situation, but he can restore and use the brokenness too. Nothing is wasted in his hands.

the first things Scripture tells us—God saw Adam wandering around the garden of Eden all alone and said, "That's not good." In Genesis 2:18, God said, "It is not good for the man to be alone, so I will create a companion for him, a perfectly suited partner" (THE VOICE).

Even in Paradise, before the fall, when things were in their perfect state and there was no sin or shame to mess things up, there was one thing that wasn't good—for man to be alone. So God created Adam's counterpart—his partner in crime and balance point. The Bible tells us, "This is the reason a man leaves his father and his mother, and is united with his wife; and the two become one flesh" (Genesis 2:24 THE VOICE).

Let's repeat that last part: The *two* become *one.* Two people, created uniquely, coming together as one. Two equals one isn't our equation; it's not something we came up with—it's God's equation!

This message isn't about codependency—Adam and Eve didn't change who they were or suddenly pretend to like all the same things. As we talk more about love, you will see that our differences don't have to divide us. In fact, they can bring us closer together because the equation God introduced in the garden runs deeper than our differences.

DECIDE TO WORK AS A TEAM

If you want a two-equals-one marriage, you and your spouse will have to decide whether or not you will be *for* each other. That doesn't mean always thinking alike, but it does mean thinking together. It doesn't mean you always agree, but it does mean working together as a team. A team works toward a common goal. A quarterback can have the most impressive arm in the world, but if he doesn't throw toward his receiver, the team will never score a touchdown. In the same way, if what you are doing isn't acting for your spouse, then no matter how impressive your effort might be, it won't strengthen your marriage.

The decision to be for your spouse and to work as a team has the power to transform a marriage; we know because that was our experience. As we share our story with you, we hope you will see a pattern and learn from our mistakes. When we were each living for ourselves, our marriage was miserable. But the more we learned to live *for each other*, the more we learned to serve and complement each other, the happier and healthier our marriage became.

A two-equals-one marriage means no longer two but one—no longer competing with each other but celebrating one another.

A two-equals-one marriage means no longer two but one—no longer competing with each other but celebrating one another.

TWO-EQUALS-ONE CHALLENGE

Today we want to mark this moment in your journey. We believe that you will see a difference in your marriage by walking with us—mark this point in time; later you will be able to see the progress and note the changes made.

Take a moment on your own to consider where you're at in your marriage. Then ask yourself the following questions:

- What are my goals?
- What are my concerns?
- Did I pick up this book on a whim, or have I read many marriage books in the hopes of revitalizing my relationship?
- What's coming up for me? What am I anticipating in my future?

PRAYER

Father, thank you for my spouse. I recognize that you have created us differently on purpose, and I want to discover how to embrace those differences and fully love my spouse. Help me to live for my spouse so that we can journey together. Lord, as I feel the emotions of where our marriage is currently, help me to examine my heart. Help me to see with new lenses the part I play in our marriage so that I can be whole and healthy. Please give me the courage to face each obstacle as it comes. In Jesus' name, amen.

CHAPTER TWO

LOVING YOUR DIFFERENCES

Your differences can become
your strengths.

Was it easier to love your spouse back when you were dating than it is now that you're married? Is the person you pledged your life to more difficult to do life with than you anticipated? Maybe you're a few years in, or a few kids later, and the stress of life has made your differences something you now can't stand.

If this sounds familiar, you're not alone. We meet with couples all the time who tell us that they feel as if "the magic is gone."

When you're dating or just starting your life together, the differences are exciting. No one wants to date a carbon copy of themselves. That would be so boring! You want someone you can't predict, who surprises you and challenges you. Someone who is strong where you are not and someone who makes you feel secure where you otherwise would feel insecure.

We all know the adage "Opposites attract." It would be more accurate, though, to say, "Opposites attract . . . until they don't."

The "feeling" that Hollywood wants us to believe is love isn't reliable. In real life that feeling can be easily disrupted. Just think of the last time your spouse annoyed you—you probably weren't feeling fireworks in that moment. Maybe you're not "feeling" it right now in your marriage. That pattern in his life you used to love is annoying now. Or that habit of hers you used to say was cute now makes you angry. The "feeling" isn't what it was in the beginning.

REAL TALK

Jimmy

I've been preaching for nearly three decades, and I've seen a number of unforgettable moments throughout the years. One of the most memorable happened at a youth conference back in 1997. I was the same fiery, passionate preacher I am today—just younger!

Every time I stepped onto that platform, my goal was the same: to inspire and to change lives. But on this particular evening, I would be the one to leave changed. The service went great, but it was the conversation I had offstage that moved me. You see, I was single at the time, and I won't lie, I was routinely scoping and hoping—scanning everywhere for my potential wife. That night after I walked offstage, a lady approached me and said that she had a word for me, which is church talk meaning that God spoke to her about me while I was preaching. She didn't know me or my situation, but what she said was exactly what I needed to hear.

She was smiling, but her tone was serious: "Stop looking for your wife. God is going to send her, and she is going to love everything that is different about you."

Now, for most people, hearing this once probably would've been enough, but this was actually the second time God had sent me this word. He used two different youth conferences and two different women, both with the same message. I guess I'm not always the best listener! But this time I was done running, and I was ready to listen. I stopped scanning everywhere I went and started trusting that God would bring her to me.

My day job was working as an IT recruiter, and, sure enough, a few months after the conversation at that youth conference, the company hired a new recruiter named Irene. I was so taken with her in that skirt and those heels that I asked our manager if I could be unofficially in on the interview process so that I could meet her. She moved into the cubicle a couple over from mine, and the first time I saw her, I knew. I made it my mission to recruit her—not for IT, but for life.

Cubicle walls are thin, so before you go accusing me of snooping, it wasn't hard to overhear conversations in that office building. One day I overheard Irene on the phone with her sister. "I'm tired of this dating game," she said. "I'm looking for someone to settle down with." From what I gathered, she had just broken up with her boyfriend and was venting to her sister. That window was all I needed!

Before she hung up the phone, I was at her desk. "I'll call you back," she told her sister, eyeing me curiously. I leaned casually on the wall of her cubicle to show off my six-foot-three frame. I was confident, charming, and smooth, and I wasted no time—I asked her out on the spot.

"I don't date my coworkers," she said, and I could tell she meant it.

Challenge accepted.

Sometimes persistence is the most persuasive tactic, and I was determined. Eventually she agreed to go on a date, and it was incredible. It was my goal to impress her, so I planned a unique stop at the Baltimore Aquarium. Afterward we went to dinner, and I ordered a bunch of different foods, made her laugh, and asked sincere questions about her story. Then, after dinner, we wandered around the Baltimore harbor. We walked for hours, and the conversation flowed more naturally with her than with any other person I had ever talked to. We were laughing and singing, sharing stories about our lives. I'm not trying to brag, but I planned and executed the most perfect date in the history of dating.

That night when I dropped her off, I planted a kiss on her forehead. Not a real kiss, because I wanted to show her that I was for real, that I was pursuing her for the right reasons. Honestly, I felt weightless as I walked back to my car—this was 100 percent the girl I was supposed to marry.

Irene

I was honestly a little surprised I had agreed to go out with a coworker. Workplace breakups are notoriously messy, and the last thing I was looking for was more drama in my life. But as I stood there staring at myself in the mirror, surrounded by a selection of rejected first-date outfits, I couldn't help thinking how different Jimmy seemed from my previous boyfriends. *Maybe he really is different . . .*

That night at dinner he managed to check all my boxes. I love trying new things, and the table was filled with food I had never even heard of. He asked penetrating questions that made me feel seen, and he genuinely wanted to know my answers. He was vulnerable in discussing boundaries that were really important to him; he even told me that he didn't want to have sex before marriage, which blew my mind. I was new in the faith, and I'd had no idea someone with standards that high could exist.

Our chemistry was undeniable. As we wandered underwater hallways of coral reefs and shark tanks, the setting felt as surreal as the connection. I remember walking around the Baltimore harbor that evening and it feeling so natural that we would laugh or sing in public together. I kind of forgot anyone else was there. I'm typically more reserved, and his charisma and larger-than-life personality made me feel shielded, as though I didn't have to carry the conversation or work to be charming. I could just be me and enjoy all these new experiences, knowing that he was more than capable of navigating them while simultaneously making me feel special.

We were without doubt from different worlds, but I loved that—it made him that much more interesting, and it made me that much more intentional in my questions. That night when he dropped me off, without even really thinking about it, I playfully poked him in the shoulder and said, "I love everything that is different about you." I had no idea I was repeating the word spoken over him months earlier. He looked at me with tears in his eyes and asked, "What did you just say?"

This wasn't luck or a chance meeting at work—we were meant for each other. And we both knew it.

The next day on the phone with Jimmy, I confessed that I had fallen in love with him in one day.

It truly was a whirlwind romance. We were married within the year.

I loved everything different about Jimmy, and he loved everything different about me. It was actually the differences that made us so compatible. He was strong where I wasn't; where I was strong, he needed me.

But life isn't like a children's storybook, and Jimmy and I didn't go on to live "happily ever after."

So how did we go from falling in love to falling out? How did two people so perfectly fit for each other become like strangers? How did we go from embracing everything different about each other to having secret addictions and hidden agendas?

In a word: *differences.*

It's ironic, isn't it? The same recipe for romance can also wreak havoc. When Jimmy and I jumped headlong into marriage, life came at us fast. We moved into our beautiful home, built a church, and started a family. We were running so fast and leaning on each other so hard that instead of recognizing our differences, we started ignoring them. We pushed them aside as if we could compartmentalize them. The tasks of life, ministry, kids, and so on took precedence over the health of our marriage. None of those things should be neglected, but in focusing solely on them, we failed to see each other, which meant that the things we were doing often frustrated each other. Because of our unique personalities and life experiences, we tended to view things in completely different ways, no matter what we were doing. And at the pace we were trying to maintain, we didn't have the time or the energy to address any of it.

> It's ironic, isn't it? The same recipe for romance can also wreak havoc.

The littlest things could spark an argument because they were often just another example of our not seeing each other.

We were both being pulled in a million directions, mostly away from each other. Even things I was doing that were good, such as mothering our children, could make Jimmy feel resentful because of how I poured my energy into them and not him. I loved watching Jimmy preach, but again, resentment grew because of the investment he made in ministry and not me.

In those early years we allowed the adrenaline of running a church and raising kids to fuel us. But the more we focused on those roles, the more we neglected the roles of husband and wife, and the chemistry we'd felt in the beginning began to feel like friction . . . something we both resented but desperately wanted to fix.

At first our differences drew us together like the heat of passion. Eventually it felt like we got burned by them.

No one warned us about that possibility, and we had spent all our energy planning a wedding without much thought for preparing for marriage. We weren't anywhere near emotionally equipped to handle the hardship, betrayal, death, transitions, change, and all the other stressors that come with life. We went from agreeing to arguing, from delighting in the differences to detesting them.

> **At first our differences drew us together like the heat of passion. Eventually it felt like we got burned by them.**

Loving our differences isn't something we were ever taught, so we were completely unequipped to handle this shift. It was like getting lost with no map. You know you're not where you want to be, but you're so far off track that you can't even remember where you were.

Was this really how marriage was supposed to be?

RESENTMENT: THE SILENT KILLER

Differences will eventually cause division—it's totally natural. But this division gets dangerous when we don't work to reconcile, because then the door is left wide open for resentment. In Scripture, James contrasted wisdom and understanding with resentment. He cautioned against allowing bitterness to lead you to being "false to the truth" (James 3:14 ESV). Resentment presents a false reality. Resentment isn't always loud; it doesn't always involve cursing. Resentment is often a silent killer.

When we feel as though we've been wronged, we typically withdraw emotionally or have less empathy for our spouse. The internalized feelings cause us to misplace emotions or blame. They present us with a skewed version of reality.

Resentment allows your pain to project the problem onto your partner.

This is why James cautioned against letting bitterness distort the truth and Paul called bitterness a poison (Ephesians 4:31 THE VOICE).

Resentment allows your pain to project the problem onto your partner. Eventually resentment can build to the point that it destroys and can lead to divorce.

There are many reasons that marriages end in divorce: different sexual appetites, different parenting styles, different dietary preferences, or even different lifestyle priorities. But, in the end, differences such as these are usually listed under the same heading: *irreconcilable differences*.

The question then becomes this: Is it possible to reconcile your differences?

The answer, we believe, is yes. Today our marriage is stronger than ever! And your relationship can be more than sparks and the starry-eyed romance of your dating years. You can learn to love your spouse on a level that's deeper and more intimate than circumstances or seasons dictate. In fact, the seasons of life can strengthen you if you learn to navigate your differences.

Think of it like this: Differences can be like a drummer playing in the wrong time signature. If you know anything about music, you know that you first learn to play in a simpler four-beats-per measure style. But more sophisticated music requires more mature and developed rhythmic patterns. Jazz, for example, has nearly endless variety.

Love is like this. The early phases of love feel pretty effortless, but if you want to go deeper, if you want your marriage to truly sing, you have to be willing to put in the work.

The starting point, however, might surprise you. It's tempting to ignore each other's differences or gloss over them. That's what we did. But if you want to reconcile them, you have to do the exact opposite. You and your spouse need to identify all the differences that are causing disruption in your marriage and face them head-on. We're talking about the differences in your upbringings and your innate differences (the way God created each of you) as well as the different experiences that shaped your modes of thinking.

If you want your marriage to truly sing, you have to be willing to put in the work.

If you don't face these, they will have power over you because they will undermine every argument. They will become areas you subconsciously avoid so as to maintain the synthetic peace—the peace you've artificially created for the sake of avoiding an argument. What we didn't know during those early years in our marriage is that you can't connect out of a deficit. The lack of understanding—the void in your relationship—will hinder connection until you confront it and learn to love your differences. Your differences can become your strengths. You will be able to help your spouse navigate areas they lack, but only when you recognize and learn to love each other's differences.

THREE QUESTIONS TO IDENTIFY YOUR DIFFERENCES

We're not master puzzlers. The most intense puzzle we've put together was probably a thousand pieces. And it took all afternoon! The tricky part of this puzzle was that it was an "escape room" puzzle, so the picture on the front of the box wasn't the end result. On top of that,

You will be able to help your spouse navigate areas they lack, but only when you recognize and learn to love each other's differences.

the puzzle was very dark, and the images on the pieces were hard to make out. It made assembling the puzzle nearly impossible. Without knowing what the picture was supposed to be or being able to match the individual pieces, we struggled.

We see this all the time in marriages. We'll sit down for a coaching session with a couple and it doesn't take long before it becomes obvious that they're trying to reconcile differences they didn't even know they had. Like the puzzle, marriage is tricky enough when you can see where the pieces fit, but it's nearly impossible when you can't. The first step is to identify your differences—to make sense of the pieces.

To be clear, we're not talking about preferences. Preferences are things such as choosing between chicken or steak for dinner, whether to watch an action or a comedy movie, or where to go for vacation. Preferences can cause minor annoyances, but differences are much more important to discuss because differences can ultimately destroy a marriage. We want to give you three questions that can help you identify the proverbial puzzle pieces for your marriage.

Question 1: How Do You Handle Conflict?

Think about the last argument you had. What was your immediate reaction? Did you feel angry? Afraid? Did you get loud or did you internalize your feelings?

What is your method of handling confrontation—are you quick to respond or do you avoid it? What about after conflict—are you able to release your feelings and forgive or do you carry the weight of each argument into your day?

Question 2: What Were Your Expectations When You Got Married?

When you first got married, did you anticipate any changes your spouse would make after you were married? Did you picture a certain lifestyle or have a vision in mind of what marriage should look like? Was this picture based on an example? What was your "ideal marriage" modeled after?

Question 3: What Areas of Conflict Cause You to Question Your Love for Your Spouse?

What is the argument that creates the most anxiety in your heart? What source of conflict changes how you feel toward your spouse? Be as vulnerable in your answers as possible. Your feelings can be an invaluable tool once you learn how to use them.

Fill in the blank: I love my spouse because _____.

TWO-EQUALS-ONE CHALLENGE

The challenge for today is to answer these questions and then organize your feelings using the emotions word bank and diagram that follows. This will be an independent challenge because it is imperative that you are as honest as possible with each answer. Resist the temptation to answer these questions for your spouse—don't assume what the other is thinking or feeling.

This is a time for you to evaluate your own thoughts and feelings. It is an important step in moving forward in your relationship and making progress in your marriage. The goal of the diagram below is to process and logically evaluate the differences that cause disruption in your relationship. Once you have answered each question, the diagram will give you a more concise visual of your internal feelings.

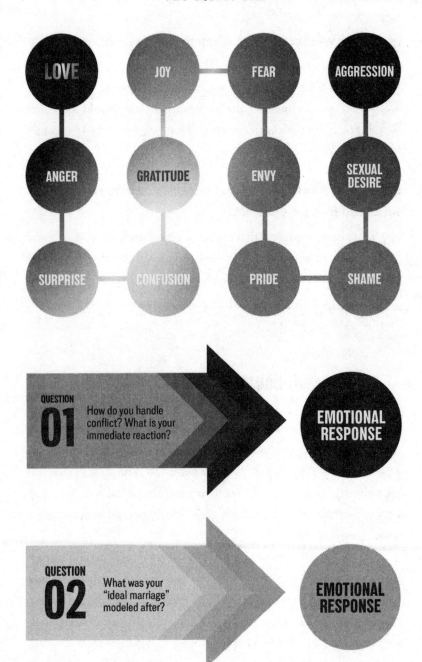

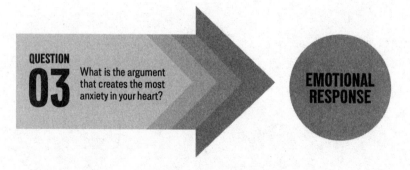

QUESTION
03
What is the argument that creates the most anxiety in your heart?

EMOTIONAL RESPONSE

PRAYER

Father, thank you for my spouse. My spouse is a gift, and I want to honor my spouse by putting in the work on our marriage. I recognize this won't be easy, but I trust that you will be with us through every struggle, disagreement, and difficult conversation. In Jesus' name, amen.

CHAPTER THREE

TURNING SECRETS INTO STRENGTHS

If you don't expose your secrets,
your secrets will expose you.

What secret have you been keeping from your spouse?
What if we told you that your secret is an opportunity for greater intimacy?

The truth is, we all have secrets. Sometimes we get it twisted and think we're keeping a secret to protect our spouse, when in reality it's hurting them. But we can reframe the way we think about them.

We are going to help you understand the truth about secrets, because they're harmful, not harmless. We suffered too long not to write about the freedom on the other side of the pain.

It's time to expose the truth about secrets: if you don't expose your secrets, your secrets will expose you.

REAL TALK

Irene

"Am I an alcoholic?"

Not long after Jimmy gave me that ultimatum, I was sitting cross-legged with my computer on my lap, glass of wine in hand, glancing over my shoulder even as I typed those words into the Google search engine. In my mind I was a master at covering my tracks. I thought I kept my secret guarded well; I thought my family had no idea how bad my drinking had gotten. I'd have a few glasses of wine while making dinner but then rush upstairs to brush and gargle before the kids got home. I'd be smiling, smelling like Listerine, and putting on a performance for Jimmy and the kids to convince them I was fine, all the while wondering, *Where can I get my next drink? How can I make sure my family doesn't find out?*

I wasn't just faking it out in public, I was putting on a front at home. And it was exhausting. I'd be asking my kids about their day but simultaneously thinking about alcohol. I wanted to be present, but addictions have a way of stealing the spotlight—when you're addicted, all other "wants" take second place.

I had a secret.

And it was making our family sick.

If you've ever kept a secret, you know that most secrets have layers. They're complicated. For me, juggling being a wife, mother, and pastor had me feeling as though I wasn't enough. My life was complicated, and I had a lot of responsibility on my shoulders. And, frankly, that helped me justify or rationalize my drinking—I'd tell myself I was busy and stressed, that "I just needed to take the edge off."

My whole life, my vocation, was built on preaching about freedom and helping people break through in their lives, so it felt as though if I shared my own struggles, it would undermine everything I stood for. I couldn't admit to the congregation, I couldn't admit to my family, and, truly, I couldn't admit to myself that I had a problem.

That evening on my laptop, asking Google for advice, was the closest I had come to admitting there was an issue. Now, a quick pastoral word: If you have to google "Am I an alcoholic?" it's probably time to talk to someone and get help. I personally let my secret keep me in a spiral of shame for way too long. It's not worth it—there is healing, you can get free. I go further into my story and how to work through addictions in my book *Reframe Your Shame*. You can experience freedom from what holds you back, but it starts with recognizing that shame is keeping you stuck. And shame was keeping us stuck in our marriage.

Think again about Adam and Eve. God created two individuals to be united as one. But then Adam and Eve disobey God and bring sin into the world. What I find so interesting is their immediate response when they realize what they've done. They don't confess. They don't even stick together when God asks them about their mistake. Adam and Eve run and hide, then proceed to blame one another (Genesis 3:7–13).

Why?

What motivated them to turn on each other?

In a word: *shame*.

Shame is the reason we keep secrets from each other. Deep down we have a fear of being rejected or abandoned. Shame whispers in our ears, telling us that if others knew our secrets, they would leave or stop loving us. When we lack awareness about how to handle this emotion, many of us do exactly what Adam and Eve did—we hide.

Jimmy and I were great at putting on a front and making ourselves look the part. This is something we all learn at a young age. It's not always a bad thing, because sometimes it's necessary. You can't go around telling everyone everything about yourself! But problems arise when you run and hide from your spouse. You can't have a two-equals-one marriage without honesty and transparency—Adam and Eve are the "what not to do." The design God created requires vulnerability. It requires honesty because truth brings us together.

I was holding on to the lie and hiding my secret from Jimmy. Consequently, our marriage was suffering.

Jimmy

"Where should we go for date night?"

The wrong restaurant can ruin a date night, so location is an important decision. Irene and I love going out—it's one of many ways we've learned to keep the spark alive. We'll talk about this more later, but in this case date night revealed some of our cracks that were quickly becoming craters.

There was a several-month stretch when Irene's answer was consistently "Let's get some Mexican food tonight." Now, I can get down with Mexican food, so I was all in the first few times she recommended it. But eventually it started to get old. I had so many amazing options I wanted to try; I couldn't understand why we weren't diversifying. From my limited perspective I just assumed I had married someone with a disproportionate love of tacos.

It wasn't until Irene was ready to talk about her problem that she worked up the courage to explain that she chose Mexican food because it was a convenient excuse to get margaritas; it was the tequila, not the tacos. And the reason she would always use the restroom right after we ordered was to sneak over to the bar to tell the waiter to add an extra shot to hers.

I had suspicions—I wasn't clueless—but I had no idea how bad the secret really was. It was silently sneaking into our marriage and wreaking havoc on it.

But she wasn't the only one with secrets. I had my own too.

The pressure of leading a growing church, being present for my kids, and working on our shaky marriage was too much to handle at times. Food had become my vice. What once was a source of joy and fun for me had become a crutch. While Irene ate to live, I lived to eat. Everything became about the next meal—the unhealthier, the better. Eventually it got so bad that I couldn't hide it anymore. I was tipping the scales at 420 pounds, and the doctors were telling me that unless something changed, I was in danger. But I couldn't stop; I had an addiction, and although it was obvious and Irene knew it, she didn't know why. She didn't know that food was my coping mechanism, a way I could push down the pain I was trying to stifle.

Food was my secret, and the thing about secrets is that they separate us. They come between us and drive us apart. But it doesn't have to be that way—secrets hinder us only until we are willing to discuss them. When we know how to be honest with our spouse about our secrets, not only do we disarm the secrets, but we can actually draw closer because of them.

My overeating initially formed a wedge between Irene and me, but once I learned how to be honest with her about it, it became an opportunity to invite Irene into the deeper places of hurt and pain in my life. My issue became an opportunity for growth in our marriage. But I had to get real with her—I had to talk to her about the pain beneath the surface that I was trying to numb with each meal.

My secret became an opportunity for deeper intimacy, which is a crucial component of the two-equals-one marriage equation. So often we equate intimacy with sex, and although that's a big part of it, it's more than that. Intimacy means letting your spouse into every aspect of your life.

Intimacy. Read that out loud. *In-to-me-see.*

If you want to have a two-equals-one marriage, you have to be willing to show your spouse everything. Your whole self—even your secrets. The courage to be honest is healing in a marriage.

My battle with pornography is another example of this. Food

wasn't my only secret struggle; in my lower moments, porn has drawn me in. It's not something I ever wanted in my life. From a young age I knew it was wrong and that it was holding me back from the life God had for me. When I was a young man and not yet married, I felt ashamed, as though I were letting down God and the church. But that shame was nothing compared to what I felt once I was married.

You see, I had been under the illusion that marriage would fix my problem. I use the word *illusion* on purpose—an illusion is a trick that appears real or true but isn't. I thought that once I was in a committed relationship, I wouldn't be tempted by porn anymore. At first this illusion seemed true, but like any trick, it lasts only a moment. It wasn't long before I found myself stumbling again, only this time the list of who I was disappointing included my wife.

The shame was overwhelming. There was a void in my life, and I was ashamed of admitting it—and of what that might mean. So instead of looking deeper into my emotions or considering what these feelings might be telling me, I went looking to fill the void. Most would probably assume that I was fantasizing about strippers or dark-web fetishes, but, in truth, I was searching housewife fantasies. I was searching in all the wrong places for what I felt I was lacking in real life.

The shame told me that I had to keep this part of me a secret. While in my mind I was protecting Irene by keeping this secret, in reality I was hurting her. The longer I put off this conversation, the greater the divide became between us.

There were times when I attempted to share the void I was feeling—to express the disconnect between us. I remember one time in particular when we were only a couple of years into our marriage. Sitting next to her on St. Stephen's Pier, over a crab cake, I confided that I had become emotionally involved with a female friend—to the point that, although I had never acted physically on it, I felt unfaithful to Irene. You see, infidelity doesn't always require action, and it isn't always sexual. But in those early years, despite our genuine efforts, Irene and I could only ever seem to patch over our issues and never fully repair anything.

By the time Irene and I hit rock bottom, the secrets had accrued like a debt we couldn't pay. Like a pile of bills hitting your desk stamped "overdue." The conversations we had avoided for so long hadn't gone away like we had thought they would. It didn't look or feel as though we had any chance of reconciling these issues. But years later while in counseling, when I finally shared my struggle with pornography, Irene's response was healing.

Sure, initially she was shocked. There was silence and confusion at first. But she didn't get angry; she didn't walk out. She responded in love; she responded out of what I needed, not what she felt. Instead of pushing me away, she entered into the fight with me and began to help me identify the driving forces that pushed me toward porn. She became a bridge to my healing, not a blockade.

REFRAME YOUR SECRETS

Your marriage will always be as sick as your secrets. That was certainly true for us. If you want to have a two-equals-one marriage, you have to be honest and vulnerable. But it's not easy; it involves intentional work. We all tend to put up walls—to make a defense around ourselves— but that ends up being an obstacle to vulnerability with your spouse.

It's important to note that when we have these conversations, we are intentional about being aware of and disarming our own walls, because unless we're willing to change, these conversations will get us nowhere. When having honest and vulnerable conversations, the goal is to grow and become closer—it's not about "winning."

We are going to help you reframe secrets as an opportunity for intimacy. Every secret you keep from your spouse is a missed opportunity for intimacy because secrets act like a wall in relationships. The more walls you put up, the more your marriage will suffer. But the more transparent we are, the greater our marriage becomes.

THREE HARD TRUTHS ABOUT SECRETS

We want to help you step into greater intimacy by giving you three hard truths about the sickness of secrets and then equipping you with some practical tools to help you have real talk.

Truth 1: Secrets Create Insecurity in Your Spouse

One thing we both discovered through these honest conversations was that neither one of us was an Oscar-worthy actor. We may have fooled others who didn't know us well, but we hadn't truly fooled one another. There's a very good chance your spouse has suspicions. The problem with suspicions is that until you have all the facts or the full story, you can come up with a whole script in your head that only makes the distance grow.

Every secret you keep from your spouse is a missed opportunity for intimacy.

We did this to one another. Instead of sharing, for example, about the alcohol or the pornography, we covered it up. This led us each to think we were the problem—I thought that Irene was drinking to be intimate because I wasn't enough or that she was just that miserable in our marriage. In the addiction world, this is referred to as "crazy making." It's the cover-up that throws others off and allows them to assume the blame, thereby making them feel as though they're crazy to even have suspicions. Crazy making causes others to question themselves and their suspicions rather than the one with the addiction. It's when, instead of engaging in honest conversation regarding our spouse's concerns or suspicions, we throw them off by making them feel bad for their questions.

We have a genuine Enemy, friends. And secrets are his playground. He will use them every time until you are dizzy from the carousel of lies.

The crazy making isn't just frustrating, it's destructive. And the lies generate insecurity—any breakdown in trust naturally creates insecurity between two people. Lies draw an invisible line in a marriage. When you have a hidden habit or a harmful pattern in life, it doesn't just weigh on you; it creates a division between you and the person you are closest to.

The questions you must ask are: Do I love my spouse enough to be honest with them? Do I love my spouse enough to stop letting my secrets cause insecurity in their life?

Truth 2: Secrets Don't Just Go Away

One of the biggest lies about marriage is that it will fix all your problems. Anyone who has been married longer than a few days knows that is not true.

In fact, marriage will magnify your problems, because now you're dealing with two sets of issues rather than one. And two sets of issues have to figure out how to consolidate, or they will surely suffocate. If you're about to be married but have a secret addiction, don't think that somehow saying "I do" to this person will suddenly make you able to say "I don't" to your addiction. You will be the same broken person in your marriage as you are now.

Instead, get help now.

Talk to someone today.

Put in the work beforehand.[1]

Maybe you've been married a long time and you've been hoping your secret will just disappear. You stuff it down, try to bury it deep. You've kept it this long, you reason; bringing it up now would be worse . . . too late now, right?

Unfortunately, secrets don't just go away. In his letter to the church at Galatia, Paul wrote, "A man reaps what he sows" (Galatians 6:7). In church that verse is often used as a positive example—you will reap generously after your hard work. While that is true, the same principle applies to the negative things we sow as well. Secrets are like weeds; if you don't pull them up with the roots, they will keep coming back. It's only a matter of time. The longer they linger, the more they're able to spread into other areas of your life.

Are you willing to do the hard work? To talk to someone about the thing you keep hidden? To bring your secret out of the corner of your heart and into the light where you can heal?

Truth 3: Weakness Is an Opportunity to Grow in Love

If you couldn't tell, we are on a mission to help you and your spouse reframe your secrets. When you admit the things that you are afraid to talk to your spouse about, your intimacy will grow.

But only if you are also growing in love.

The Bible makes clear that without love, nothing else really matters. In 1 Corinthians 13:2, Paul said, "If I had such faith that I could move mountains, but didn't love others, I would be nothing" (NLT). Sometimes we need to be reminded of this, whether we've grown so comfortable or we're just so busy that we stop seeing that person we chose for life.

Love is a decision: As a married couple, we have to decide to remain a team. This means that we have to decide to welcome each other's shortcomings rather than shut them out or judge them. This means we need to be as intentional in our love as we are in our honesty.

But resentment can be sneaky. It's like being bitten by a mosquito—you don't usually know you've been bitten until it starts to itch. It's the same with resentment; you may not even remember exactly what happened, but you'll remember the way your spouse made you feel and it'll start to itch. Resentment plagued our marriage even early on. We have always been open to counseling and even went together before we were married, but resentment significantly hindered our progress.

Maybe you can relate. You feel as though you've been doing the work, you've been going to counseling or trying your hardest, but you feel stuck. Everyone's equation for marriage is going to look a bit different—your obstacle may not be obvious at first and you may have more than one to overcome. For us, a major strain on our relationship was built-up, unexpressed resentment that acted like a barricade between us and intimacy.

Isn't it crazy how you can withhold love from your spouse out of resentment while at the same time withholding a secret from them yourself?

Secrets and resentment share quite a bit of common ground, and they both keep you from what you want. Resentment will tell you to place blame where it doesn't belong, but that won't resolve the source of your frustration. We often keep secrets thinking that our relationship will be better off if we don't share that part of ourselves, but instead it only creates distance between us.

> **Isn't it crazy how you can withhold love from your spouse out of resentment while at the same time withholding a secret from them yourself?**

Sometimes love can be messy. When we become our spouse's true confidant—the one they are most vulnerable and honest with—we have a sacred trust, and sometimes that trust means being the one picking the other up when they fall. Without love large enough to cover each other, we don't have a shot at intimacy.

Think about the apostle Paul, a giant of the Christian faith. He had a thorn in his flesh, something holding him back (2 Corinthians 12:7). Something I'm sure he would have rather kept a secret. This man planted many churches and is estimated to have written between 25 and 50 percent of the New Testament. By any standard, he is a legend; so don't you think he would rather not divulge a weakness to the same churches he was pastoring? But instead of hiding this hindrance, Paul wrote to the church in Corinth about it.

Why? Because he understood the power of love. He wrote, "That is why, for Christ's sake, I delight in weaknesses, in insults, in hardships, in persecutions, in difficulties. For when I am weak, then I am strong" (2 Corinthians 12:10). Paul understood that, through love, our weaknesses hold a tremendous amount of potential.

Your secret is an opportunity for you and your spouse to grow in love for each other. It may not feel like it yet, and the first time you share, it may be really hard. Some of the things you will learn to communicate with one another may take some time to process, and we'll talk more about that in the next section, but, at the end of the day, love does have the power to overcome many sins. Love is stronger.

Your secret is an opportunity for you and your spouse to grow in love for each other.

So do you love your spouse enough to create a safe place for them to share? Do they know they can be honest with you?

REAL LOVE VS. COUNTERFEIT LOVE

Real love looks a lot different from the cheap, counterfeit love that society tries to sell us. The kind of love you can offer your spouse is the kind that can transform their secret into their strength. It can cover their shortcomings and create a place where they feel safe enough to share their secrets with you.

But this honest, vulnerable, real love is going to require real talk. The kind we often avoid. I (Irene) want to share one more story to illustrate what this might look like for you.

The initial conversation and subsequent lie took root all the way back in our dating years. It was when we had the whole "body count" conversation. We were riding in the car, and somehow the subject came up. Without concern for his own response, Jimmy asked me what my number was.

Now, remember, Jimmy and I are from very different backgrounds. Jimmy was open on his stance of waiting until marriage; he was a virgin. So as soon as the subject came up, I was uncomfortable. My number was not zero. *How could I live up to that?*

Shame rose quickly, choking my voice. I felt as though I had let him down, and fear was telling me that if I told the truth, he would reject me and not want to marry me. I had to formulate a response. I lied. I made up a story and gave him a fake number.

Today I have a lot of grace for myself and my decision in the car that day. We hadn't put in the hard work required to have the difficult conversations, so I didn't feel safe telling him the truth. But that didn't stop the lie from creating tension around that issue for the next fifteen years. We missed out on an opportunity for greater intimacy for a decade and a half because I wanted to keep my secret. Because I was afraid of being seen for my past choices, the lie I told to cover up my past created a divide between us.

Fast-forward several years and we were sitting with a counselor. Even in therapy I was still so guarded. That day our counselor told Jimmy that his reaction to other people's promiscuous pasts had made it virtually impossible for me to feel safe enough to open up to him.

Something clicked for him. He turned to me and, leaning forward in his chair, said over and over, "I love you.

"I still love you.

"I'm not going anywhere.

"I just don't want any secrets between us."

It was what I needed to hear. Tears ran down my cheeks. I believed him. The love we had built over the years began to speak louder than my shame. I was ready to be honest—I was ready for real talk. I had never felt more vulnerable, but as I spoke, walls I hadn't known I had began to fall. Shame is a paralyzing emotion, and it had had a powerful hand over my mouth for years, stifling any attempts I made to tell the truth.

The Enemy wanted me to keep hiding in shame, but as soon as I spoke the truth, there was intimacy where there had once been only isolation. What I had uncovered, Jimmy covered in the same way Christ covers us. This is the love we are called to reflect. The kind of love Christ demonstrated for us—he is the ultimate example of what it means to cover sins in love.

Jimmy listened and then began to share about his past and his secrets too.

As imperfect humans, we play pointless comparison games. As if somehow figuring out who has more baggage is useful information. I want you to know that love covers a multitude of sins (1 Peter 4:8). When we learn how to love each other the way Christ loves the church, we stop playing those games. We decide to love despite each other's pasts. That's the reason the starting point for two equals one is love.

We will get into more practical information about strengthening laughter and communication and fostering longevity in your marriage—but if we don't start with love, we won't get anywhere. Love is the priority. With that in mind, take some time to reflect. Are you creating a safe place for your spouse to be vulnerable? What do you want or need to feel safe? We can't be all that God created us to be if we're resisting vulnerability and honesty with our spouse.

TWO-EQUALS-ONE CHALLENGE

Your marriage will always be as sick as your secrets. The good news is that honesty can bring healing, but before we can be honest with each other, we have to be honest with ourselves.

First, take a long, hard look and examine yourself—your secrets, wants, and unspoken needs. Pray and be honest and vulnerable with God. Is there something you've been keeping from your spouse? An addiction you've been covering up? A moment from your past that you've been too ashamed to talk about? Or maybe a dream that you've been keeping to yourself?

Real talk begins with you. If you want to create a safe place where you and your spouse can be honest and vulnerable, you have to be willing to do the work on yourself first.

Once you are able to be honest with yourself, write a list of things that you have been withholding that you want to share with your spouse. If you have a more serious confession, we recommend you talk to a marriage counselor first. Consider bringing a paid professional in to help guide the process and facilitate conversation.

PRAYER

Father, thank you for my spouse. We are both broken, just broken differently. I'm sorry for any way in the past that I have made it difficult for my spouse to share the secrets they are holding on to. Please give me strength and the grace needed to create a safe place in our marriage. And I pray that my spouse would know right now, at this moment, that you love them, and so do I. Replace any fear with love. In Jesus' name, amen.

CHAPTER FOUR

COMPLEMENTING, NOT COMPLETING

You don't complete each other.
You complement each other.

There's a reason people say "opposites attract." Oftentimes we look to our spouse to fulfill something we missed in our childhood, to fill a void that otherwise might cause us insecurity or even pain. This is by design. After all, we exist to bring out the best in each other! Sometimes even differences that are painful to address, things you would never have anticipated being a weakness in yourself, are strengths you find in your spouse.

Learning to celebrate each other's differences not only can unite you but can actually reveal your true selves. Our differences are a beautiful gift God gives us. In the same way that Eve was the perfect complement to Adam, each spouse can help the other become the best version of themselves. Yes, you can dominate your differences when you realize that they aren't meant to destroy your marriage. In fact, they can bring unity to your marriage through the beauty of diversity.

REAL TALK

Irene

A few years ago, Ian Morgan Cron invited me to be a guest on his *Typology* podcast. Ian is a master teacher of the Enneagram, a personality test that helps us understand ourselves and each

You can dominate your differences when you realize that they aren't meant to destroy your marriage.

other. His show is full of interesting conversation about life and relationships, and he's known for his challenging questions.

I was fairly new to podcasting and a bit nervous, so as we were wrapping up, I was silently applauding myself for staying close to the mic and keeping my note cards in order. That's when Ian looked at me through his thick-rimmed glasses and challenged my entire thesis.

"Is it really helpful to view marriage through the lens of two equals one?" he asked. "Isn't the point of the journey the differentiation?"

He's right . . . what's the difference between codependency and two equals one?

Brief moment of panic, and then it clicked. I might've been a rookie podcast guest with a thin line of sweat running down my spine, but I had the chance to make a very important distinction.

It's true that there is a codependent way to approach this equation for marriage, especially when one spouse overpowers the other. Two equals one could turn into one spouse running the entire show, while the other lays down all the things that make them different and unique in an attempt to appease the other. But that's not the true version of the equation.

The true version of two equals one is an invitation to love everything that is different about your spouse. "Two equals one is two completely different, separate human beings with completely different giftings, talents, and wounds coming together as one," I told him.

I went on to explain that coming together means leveraging your differences. It's not about enabling each other but empowering one another. Your differences don't have to create resentment and separation; they can bring you together. That turned the whole conversation.

> **The true version of two equals one is an invitation to love everything that is different about your spouse.**

Jimmy

In the New Testament, the Gospels record the story of a woman with an "issue of blood" (Luke 8:43–48 KJV). Scholars believe she had a hemorrhage, and what that meant for this woman was isolation. According to Jewish law, she would have been considered "unclean," and, furthermore, anyone who came in contact with her would have become unclean as well. Scripture tells us she had been bleeding for twelve years.

One day Jesus passed near her in a crowd, and if you know the story, you know that she reached out and touched Jesus and was immediately healed. What happened next is easy to miss because it seems like the miracle should get the most attention, right? But Jesus made a point of stopping when everyone else would have kept on walking through the crowded street, and he asked, "Who touched me?" (Luke 8:45). You can almost hear his disciples' tone when they referred to the bustling crowds pressing in on all sides, but Jesus insisted. Jesus stopped. *Who touched me?*

This woman now had a choice—she'd already gotten her miracle. She could walk away healed.

But instead, she confessed.

This woman did the unthinkable—she touched Jesus in an unclean state and now, likely for the first time in twelve years, she was in the middle of an enormous crowd of people . . . and she confessed.

Don't miss what Jesus told her: "Daughter, your faith has made you well; go in peace, and be healed of your disease" (Mark 5:34 ESV).

Confession and honest, open communication earned her the title of "daughter." She was seen in that moment—vulnerable and known. Instead of being condemned, she was praised. Instead of receiving judgment, she received freedom, but it took the courage to confess.

Being seen can be scary, but it's the only way to be known. Until we are willing to be honest in relationships, especially with God and with our spouse, we can't expect to be seen. We can't expect to be fully known.

You might be thinking, *How does this relate to me? Some random, unnamed woman in Scripture who was healed of a physical, internal, uncommon hemorrhage—what does that have to do with my story?* Maybe you're a man and you're thinking, *She's not even married. How does this connect to me?*

The answer, frankly, is *everything*.

Let's put it like this: In war zones, injuries from shrapnel are common. Shards of metal are flung from a bomb or a land mine, and unfortunately most victims are innocent civilians. What you may not realize is that the actual injury, the torn flesh or damage from this debris, is not usually the cause of death. The most common way that shrapnel kills is sepsis—an infection that manifests only later, after the shard has lingered in the body.[1] It won't be a visible bleeding or a wound that is clearly identified—it's an internal injury that grows when left untreated.

We all have wounds. We've all caught some metaphorical shrapnel in our lifetime that has left us internally scarred. It may not be obvious to everyone, but I'm willing to bet your wound is bleeding into other areas of your life. Maybe it manifests as anger in your home or a deafening silence where there used to be open communication. We all have issues—things that we're ashamed of, that we hide from others. But those things don't go away just because we aren't willing to deal with them.

I want you to pause here.

Consider what your shrapnel may be.

What caused the invisible wound you so carefully conceal?

Consider why you might be stuffing the pain rather than speaking it.

Consider that if you're hiding something, you may be hurting someone.

Maybe you've been told that you just need to have more faith—that you're the reason you're suffering. I've heard that one a time or two! The woman in this story was probably told the same thing. She was probably also told that her disease was a result of sin, that it was punishment for her own wrongdoing or the result of someone else's. Sound familiar? Sometimes we let others diagnose us, and it leads us down a path of managing pain rather than healing. The person we let diagnose us may have caused the injury in the first place.

Now, I'm not saying that we never deal with consequences that are of our own making—I've certainly done my share of wrong! But whatever the cause of the wound, hiding it only allows the sepsis to take hold. And, my friend, that kind of infection doesn't just kill your marriage—it can take you out altogether.

So how do we treat these invisible injuries? In a word: *confession.* Jesus made a point of asking "Who touched me?" not because he didn't know but because he wanted to diagnose her. You see, up until this point, she had been known only by her issue. She's literally known throughout the Gospels only as "the woman with the issue of blood." But this was not how Jesus referred to her. No one in that crowd knew her as anything other than her disease. They didn't know her as "daughter." Her affliction had interfered with every relationship in her life—isolating her to the point that no one even saw her that day. Only Jesus, and only when she confessed.

That day her trauma became her testimony.

That day, through having the courage to confess, she laid claim to a new identity. Her identity had already changed—she was healed. But she had to claim it in order to be known. Known as "daughter."

This is how love works: Something must die for God's love to live. In this case it was her old identity. For some, it might be an expectation that needs to die or a want that you keep placing over the needs of your spouse.

Loving everything that's different about your spouse is a different kind of love—*we have to be willing to let the old version of love die in order to claim the kind of love God demonstrates!*

Friend, I want you to know that you are a child of God. God loves you too much to leave you wounded. But you have to receive your new identity, and the only way to do so is to come out of hiding—out of isolation. We can't self-diagnose this—we can't WebMD our symptoms and fix ourselves. Scripture tells us the woman in our story spent everything she had and that she was still in tremendous pain.

Loving everything that's different about your spouse is a different kind of love— we have to be willing to let the old version of love die in order to claim the kind of love God demonstrates!

God wants so much more for you!

If it's not good, God is not done.

But you have to be willing to claim the testimony on the other side of your trauma.

YOU COMPLEMENT EACH OTHER

Every once in a while, we watch a romantic comedy together. They're entertaining and provide a two-hour break from reality. But as far as the marriage advice Hollywood has to offer, well, that's mostly trash. As a general rule, movies give terrible marital advice.

You have to be willing to claim the testimony on the other side of your trauma.

Perhaps one of the most famous romantic comedies is the smash hit *Jerry Maguire*. Jerry (Tom Cruise) falls in love with a single mother, Dorothy (Renée Zellweger). Jerry is a standard workaholic, and Dorothy prioritizes her son. The climax of the movie is a huge argument that ends with their going separate ways. But, in an iconic scene, Jerry rushes back to Dorothy, and standing dramatically in her doorway, he gives an impassioned speech in which he tells her, "You complete me."

It's a scene raw with passion and tears, and it's easy to get caught up as the music builds the moment. If we're not careful, we can start believing this concept—that our spouse exists to complete us. But when we buy into that, when we believe that's their job, we will be let down 100 percent of the time. You don't *complete* each other. You *complement* each other.

A recent study showed that 30 percent of all married couples regret their marriages because they believe they would be happier if they had married someone they were "more compatible" with.[2] This is the lie of believing your spouse "completes" you. But a loving marriage isn't about finding everything you need in another person. It actually means the opposite. It means you choose not to let your differences

You don't *complete* each other. You *complement* each other.

49

divide you. One of the most beautiful things about marriage is that it's between two people who are different from each other.

The question "Is my spouse everything I need them to be?" then becomes "How can I love everything that's different about my spouse?"

One of the most beautiful things about marriage is that it's between two people who are different from each other.

This may mean sacrificing some of your independence but not your individuality. It doesn't mean we stop being who we are to cater to our spouse; when two equals one, you find out how to become more of who you are. And your spouse is the one encouraging you to be who you are. A loving marriage is two different individuals working as a team. The day we stopped letting our differences divide us, they began to bring us together again.

This includes the trauma and the baggage. This includes your habits and hang-ups and all the broken pieces you cover up. When you allow your spouse access to what has otherwise been off-limits to others, you will find a strength you never knew.

But it starts with love. When you love someone enough that you choose them for life, it stands to reason that there are things you can learn from them—ways that they can help you become a better, more fulfilled person. The trouble is, we often don't realize how many differences we have until after marriage, and then some aren't as endearing as we used to think!

All marriages have differences. Life would be pretty boring without them! Our marriage is proof that the differences can make you stronger instead of dividing you—if you're willing to put in the work. Differences won't reconcile themselves, but with some hard work, humility, and God's formula of two equals one, all differences can be reconciled.

We have felt the distance that differences can create, to the point of a metaphorical continental divide. But it was when we stopped and took a hard look at our differences that we began a journey to reconciliation. Remember how we talked about "irreconcilable differences"? What if the differences that have you feeling so cornered and so defeated are actually designed to bring out your best? It's like a lock and key; without each other they can't be all they were designed to be. Two very different creations, but their purpose is fully realized when they work together.

TWO-EQUALS-ONE CHALLENGE

Individually, write a list of irreconcilable differences or unlovable behaviors. Do not compare notes—this is an independent exercise and is about self-reflection. Be as honest as possible in your list. What causes you the most stress or frustration? What behavior makes you feel the most neglected or ignored? What annoys you most and makes everyday life most exhausting?

Then, after you've completed your list, answer the following questions.

1. What fractures in previous relationships were you able to overcome? What were some difficult obstacles that you overcame in your past relationships? Be honest with yourself about these experiences.

2. What was irreconcilable about you that God covered? Honestly search your heart—what was the thing most undeserving about you that God redeemed? Write it down.

PRAYER

Father, thank you for my spouse. I believe you died because you loved my spouse that much. Forgive me for the times I have demonstrated a selfish love rather than the kind of love you have shown to me. Help me to love the way you do. In Jesus' name, amen.

CHAPTER FIVE

REDEFINING LOVE

Loving everything that is different about
your spouse is a different kind of love.

How would you define *love*? What comes to your mind when you think about love?

We all get our ideas of love from somewhere. Movies and music—culture is loaded with messages that we subconsciously accept as love. But love isn't what you think it is.

The Bible tells us that love doesn't come with conditions.

Love doesn't have limitations.

Love doesn't have restrictions.

If you want a two-equals-one marriage, chances are you're going to have to look at love differently. We'll look at redefining love to be the kind of love God gives us. It's not about getting from love, it's about giving. Ask yourself: Do the needs of your spouse break your heart? Are you willing to be faithful to their faults, frailties, and failures to ensure a greater future?

REAL TALK

Jimmy

A few years ago Irene and I were speaking at a marriage conference in South Carolina. Irene was five years sober, and we had been doing the work. We were at a completely different place in our lives, and specifically in our marriage, than we had ever been. This time when we were invited to speak at a marriage conference, we were ready— united. Matter of fact, we were pumped to share the wisdom we had been accumulating through our experiences.

But that day, as I looked out at the congregation, I recognized the same tense fatigue I had known for so long—the fatigue that comes from trying to hold on to appearances. You know the expression "It takes one to know one"? Well, I knew them. I had been that tired husband with a wall around my emotions.

As Irene and I sat there onstage, smiling, waiting to be introduced, I felt God prompting me inside. The pastor casually strolled over to us after introducing the other couples on the panel. Gesturing like a game-show host to his audience, he asked me, "So, Jimmy, you've been married for twenty-two years! How long have you two been in love?"

I knew he was expecting me to say a larger number—that I must have been in love with Irene before, when we were dating. But that day God demanded my honesty.

I let the question hang in the air for a moment. Swallowed hard. Then I answered, "I fell in love with Irene five years ago."

I felt the congregation lean forward, and some who were obviously doing the math in their heads were unable to contain their gasps. It was the truth. What I had called love the day we said "I do" wasn't love. And I knew distinctly the moment when my definition of love had changed.

What I had come to realize, and what God wanted me to share that day, was that my previous definition of love wasn't biblical. You see, my love had conditions—I loved Irene when life felt easy. When we weren't arguing, when we were having fun. That's what my brain associated with love. But when she became addicted to alcohol, my "love" went looking for easy. My love didn't want to deal with that. It had limits.

It was as if my "love" were a pair of designer sneakers—heaven forbid things get messy. (In fact, if it's raining, I would just as soon go barefoot as wear my Jordan OGs.) But love isn't a collector's item meant to be stored in a climate-controlled closet. Love isn't fragile or warped by hard times. It won't get ruined by the storms of life.

In 1 Corinthians, Paul wrote of three things that will outlast everything else: faith, hope, and love.

The greatest, he said, is love.

But that's not the script I had followed for the first fifteen years of our marriage.

On top of having conditions and limits, my love also made demands. It had criteria that society tells us should be met for it to be "real love." When Irene and I had differences, or it looked as if we weren't compatible, my definition of love demanded that she change. When we argued, my idea of love suggested that she should agree with me.

Like ultimatums, restrictions are rules that we put in place of relationship. They protect us, or so we think. Restrictions are our guardrails, and we think they keep us safe from personal injury, when in reality they prevent us from real love.

Real love doesn't behave this way. The phrase "love endures" occurs forty-two times in Scripture, and Paul told us point-blank that "love . . . endures *all things*" (1 Corinthians 13:7 ESV, emphasis added). The Bible gives absolutely no condition, limitation, or restriction for God's love; we are told repeatedly that it is steadfast and unfailing.

Paul said explicitly in 1 Corinthians 13 that "love never fails" (v. 8 NKJV). It never gives up.

This is the kind of love that comes from God himself, for "God is love" (1 John 4:8, 16). God's love demonstrates the ultimate sacrifice; he paid a price he didn't owe so we could have what we don't deserve.

God isn't looking at his people and waiting for the opportunity to bail. Now, let's be clear—we fail. And our mistakes and failures grieve his heart. Scripture tells us how sin affects God, and it causes him pain. We aren't blameless, but love the way God demonstrates it never gives up. He doesn't withdraw or withhold affection.

God didn't wait until we cleaned ourselves up to redeem us.

He came right in the middle of our mess.

Speaking at that marriage conference, I was moved to share our story. My heart was stirred to share what love really is—not the diluted Hollywood version of love, but real love. The love that isn't swayed by seasons of difficulty or dependent on our behavior. But, to experience real love, Irene and I had to experience pain. I'm not saying everyone has to go through the same hardships we did in order to love their spouse, but every person alive has their share of baggage.

Baggage = pain.

The life stuff that shapes us in both good and negative ways.

The question ultimately becomes whether you are willing to press into that pain and experience real love with your spouse. Are you willing to walk through the mess? Or does your "love" come with conditions?

Irene

Our marriage still exists because Jimmy was able to love me past my yuck. I'm not talking about the alcoholism, because the alcohol was an external symptom of the yuck that was going on inside me.

Have you ever watched one of those home-renovation shows?

People fall in love with a house and buy it with the intention of fixing it up; you watch them take something that has "potential" and turn it into their dream home. But what often happens during the renovation are unforeseen expenses. They run into foundation issues, plumbing problems, or faulty wiring—things that certainly weren't advertised on the listing and wouldn't have been obvious or even visible to the buyer. They're costly fixes, and it's tempting to simply cover them up. You can't see the wiring—it's behind the drywall. Cracks in the foundation are likewise camouflaged, out of sight.

But covering it up doesn't make the problem go away. Eventually faulty wiring can cause a fire. Foundation cracks lead to major issues. A homebuyer is left with the question of whether the house is worth it.

It didn't take long after Jimmy and I were married before we started noticing issues. For the most part, they weren't obvious to others. Most issues take a while to become visible—even longer before they're a full-blown threat. The Leaning Tower of Pisa was never designed to lean—it had major foundational issues from the start. Although it was completed in the fourteenth century, the threat of collapse wasn't imminent until 1990. That's when a team of engineers was brought in to reinforce and strengthen the foundation.[1]

Before you go thinking that I'm saying your marriage is good for the next seven hundred years and will become famous, the Leaning Tower of Pisa is famous for its issues. It would almost be more appropriate to say that it's an *infamous* tower. I highly doubt any of us would like that to be the descriptor of our marriage! And although the lean was visible, most people would be oblivious as to the cause or the cost to fix it.

The longer the issues remain, the costlier they become to fix—and the same is true of your marriage.

Jimmy and I have shared in small doses about some of our external indicators: alcoholism, porn, food addiction. But those weren't the foundation problems or the faulty wiring. The true issues lay beneath the surface—they're much deeper than what you can see. And, sure, those addictions needed to be addressed, but to focus solely on the external would be to put a Band-Aid on a bullet hole. It doesn't actually fix anything.

The longer the issues remain, the costlier they become to fix—and the same is true of your marriage.

Every fan of home-remodel TV shows loves demolition day. It's when the contractor or construction crew hands the unqualified homebuyers a sledgehammer and tells them to hack away at whatever section they're renovating. It's humorous to watch as the ugly obstacles to their vision for the home are blasted away . . . but if you know anything about renovation, you know that, in real life, this process is anything but carefree. As amusing as it is to watch amateurs smash things, most any internal issues will require a methodical approach to fix. There are essential steps—designing, budgeting, permitting, and so on—that might not make for entertaining reality TV, but by skipping them you could make the problems worse.

The same is true in marriage. If you rush headlong into your issues without care in your approach, you will likely cause your spouse more harm than good. You could add to the trauma or dysfunction you're experiencing.

We're going to give you tools in the next section to approach your areas of difficulty, but what this will ultimately require is love. Real love. Love that endures and never gives up. Caring for your spouse will look like having intentional conversations. Listening without agenda. Love requires us to let down our guard and be vulnerable because love rejoices at truth. Love is realizing that what needs to be redeemed in your spouse is yours to divinely care for.

Are you willing to be faithful to their faults, frailties, and failures to ensure a greater future?

CREATED FOR CONNECTION

Harvard University conducted the longest study ever on human happiness. It confirmed what the first book of the Bible recorded thousands of years ago: *it's not good for man to be alone.*

The director of the study, psychiatry professor Robert Waldinger, summarized the results, saying, "Loneliness kills. Social connections are as important to our long-term health as diet and exercise."[2]

Loneliness kills. You weren't created for isolation.

And let's be clear: You can be in a relationship, you can be married, and still feel alone—still be lonely. Connection is more than a ring on your finger. And in the same way God created Eve for Adam, you were meant to help your spouse.

When God announced that it wasn't good for man to be alone, he created Eve to be a "perfectly suited partner" (Genesis 2:18 THE VOICE). The Amplified Bible elaborates by calling her "one who balances . . . a counterpart."

A counterpart is by definition "a thing that fits another perfectly."[3] It either stands in contrast or complements, but it is never the same. You may be different from your spouse, but there is purpose in this design. If you were both the same, neither could balance the other. It is with a perfectly designed counterpart that we can grow and become the fullest version of ourselves.

By the world's math, two will always equal two. It's only through God's design that two become one. But to become one, we have to be willing to love the way God does. We read in 1 John 4:18 that "there is no fear in love, but perfect love casts out fear. For fear has to do with punishment" (ESV). Oftentimes that's exactly what's keeping us from truly loving our spouse: fear. Maybe it's a fear of what they will think or do; maybe it's a fear of rejection. Maybe we're afraid of being disappointed. There's always some type of fear associated, but whatever the fear, love calls us to more.

Some of you may have never experienced a love like this. A love that doesn't keep score. A love that grows in the hard times. A love that covers, protects, and provides a safe place. And the truth is that you can't give what you've never received.

If you don't know the kind of love we're talking about, we're talking about the love God offers, and you can experience that. He offers it freely: no conditions, limitations, or restrictions. All you have to do is pray this simple prayer:

> God, I realize that I am broken. I realize that because I am distant from you, I don't have proximity with my spouse. So, right now, I repent; I acknowledge that I am lonely without you. I confess with my mouth that I am nothing without you; life and marriage and relationships are too hard to do without you. Because of your sacrifice, I have access to your love and forgiveness. Free me, redeem me, heal me, and give me the ability to love others as you have loved me. I confess today, Jesus, that you are Lord. Thank you for saving me from me. In Jesus' name, amen.

Jimmy

One of the most frequently asked questions we get when coaching a husband or wife is "When can I leave?" Basically, they're asking "When is it okay as a Christian to get a divorce?" And, honestly, that was me.

I asked that same question.

I was that husband.

If you had asked me if my love was sacrificial, I would have likely told you that you had no idea what I had been through. What I had sacrificed for our marriage. I would have told you how I had shielded our kids and would have been able to give specific examples of the many times that I had picked up the slack.

What more could a person ask of a man than that?

At the height of Irene's drinking, I felt as though ultimatums were my only option. But even as she started to get healthy, I wasn't sure I was willing to do the work. In many ways I wanted an "out." I felt hurt and disappointed; it felt unfair. As if I were cleaning up someone else's mess.

I had so much resentment built up in my heart that I wasn't sure our marriage was worth it. My love had limits, and it felt as though that limit had been reached.

Paul said in 1 Corinthians 13:5 that love "keeps no record of wrongs," but, let me tell you, I had kept a record. I had a mental list of things that Irene had done or ways she had hurt me, ways she had failed as a wife—they were my ammunition, and they suggested a divorce was more than reasonable. That our differences were irreconcilable.

What I couldn't see then was that loving Irene wasn't about making our marriage work. It wasn't about how many years we could stay married.

God had a much bigger picture in mind.

The question I had never asked myself was *why* love keeps no record of wrongs. Psalm 103:12 says that "God takes *all* our crimes—*our seemingly inexhaustible sins*—and removes them. As far as east is from the west, *He removes them* from us" (THE VOICE). God isn't ignorant of our sins; in fact, he's the only one who has any right to judge them.

But instead of condemning us, he covers our shortcomings.

Through sacrifice—his sacrifice—he covers them.

He doesn't bring them back up or throw them in our faces.

Instead, he uses our weaknesses to display the tremendous power of his love.

What I couldn't see then was that loving Irene through the pain was actually allowing for a much greater work to be done. Our pain had a much greater purpose.

At that point in our marriage, all I understood was that God required my obedience. What I would later discover was why the list of wrongs, why the record of grievances, wasn't important. I would discover just what love can do and experience its healing power in my life.

I don't know where your marriage is today, and I don't pretend to have all the answers, but I know the One who does. I went looking for an excuse—an exception to grace, forgiveness, or hard work. Some kind of free pass that I could live with as a pastor. I found instead a God who loved relentlessly when he could have easily justified walking away. It's hard, I won't lie, and there is no caveat or free pass on doing the work in marriage. But if you don't do the work, you will miss out on the blessing.

There is a reward on the other side that comes only when you've done all you can to love. God can and will take all your dysfunction and all your issues and use them for good, but only when you're willing to live out the love that he freely gave all of us.

TWO-EQUALS-ONE CHALLENGE

Today's exercise is to independently evaluate your definitions of love. List ways that your love has conditions, limitations, and restrictions. Ask yourself these questions:

Do I choose to love my spouse even when I'm not feeling it?
Do I have limits on how much I put up with?
Do I have rules rather than relationship?

Journal your responses and evaluate whether your definition of love is influenced more by Scripture or by society. In what ways can you redefine love based on what you've been learning so far?

PRAYER

Father, thank you for my spouse. I recognize that my definition of love has not always aligned with yours. I have not always loved without condition, limitation, or restriction. Help me as I learn to love like you. In Jesus' name, amen.

PART TWO

LAUGHTER

You're probably going to wonder why we called this part "Laughter." After all, we just got done sharing how our marriage was falling apart and how many unaddressed issues were plaguing our relationship—not exactly a comedy routine! And if you're like we were, your marriage might feel at this point like a task, not a touchpoint. You're not really enjoying being married—you're enduring. The joy of the Lord is our strength, and laughter is a characteristic of joy, so if you are enduring rather than enjoying your marriage, you don't have much strength in your marriage.

A common misconception is that a relationship is strong when two people appear to be happy or life seems easy. But you don't acquire joy from strength. Many of us think that our marriage will become more joyful with more strength, but it's actually the opposite: You get more strength because you have joy. Our marriage will be stronger when we are filled with joy, but it's important here to note that joy is not a feeling.

Joy isn't the same as happiness.

Nehemiah 8:10 tells us, "The joy of the LORD is your strength." When the prophet Nehemiah told the Israelites this, the people were in mourning—they'd been convicted of their own shortcomings and failures, and they were weeping. Yet rather than allow the people to remain in this state of grief, Nehemiah admonished them to no longer mourn but instead take hold of the joy that comes from the Lord.

Joy isn't dependent on a season.

It doesn't rely on behavior or works.

Society has done a great job of creating a counterfeit to joy that shows itself in marriage most often in the form of sarcasm. We've all seen memes or reels on social media making fun of the nagging wife or the obtuse husband. You may even be smirking about one now.

The problem with sarcasm is that it is often a cry for help. When I felt hopeless in our marriage or was frustrated with Irene, this was my go-to for comedy. Sarcasm was my weapon of choice. But sarcasm doesn't come from a place of joy, and it doesn't produce strength. It's destructive—it diminishes and reduces, it weakens relationships.

You might think the only moments of laughter in your recent past have been the result of a sarcastic joke or reel on social media. Maybe you're trying to relive moments of happiness from your past or, worse, seeking to fill the void in your relationship with imitation intimacy. In our marriage we began to resent each other because we no longer felt what, in the beginning, we had recognized as love. It was at that point we stopped laughing together.

You've probably heard the adage "Anything worth having is worth working for." Not only is this true, but it's often a requirement. You can't expect to get enjoyment from something that you're not putting in the work for. In the same way that hitting every fairway in golf doesn't just happen, a lasting marriage is no accident. You can't skip past the hard stuff and expect the happily ever after.

Before you sigh in disappointment at the idea of more tasks, here's the good news: Your marriage çan bring you infinitely more enjoyment than any sport or hobby in the world. It can introduce you to yourself—your real self—but only if you're willing to do the work.

We like to say that your spouse is your blueprint for growth. What that means is that, as you come to know your spouse more and learn from them, you will naturally realize things about yourself that you never would have seen on your own. The things you share and the intimacy that grows as a result will bond you together. Your marriage can be like your own private club that no one else gets to share. Your spouse will become the person you are most comfortable with—the one person you can truly let down your guard around.

This isn't about having a social media marriage or putting on a front for those around you. This isn't about changing your status to "it's complicated" or settling for what society tells us is the "standard" for married life.

Your marriage should be about more than existing—it should make you feel excited. When we stop looking for strength in moments of happiness, when we seek the joy that comes from God and define our marriage in biblical terms rather than how the world defines marriage, our spouse becomes the person we're most able to laugh with.

And couples who laugh together stay together.

CHAPTER SIX

CRACKING THE COMMUNICATION CODE

Before you can laugh together, you
first have to learn to communicate.

How long has it been since you and your spouse laughed together?
Laughter isn't a cure-all that fixes everything in marriage,
but it's an indication of marital health. Laughter is a litmus test—it
shows whether you're on the same page. If healthy communication
is a seed you plant in the ground and nurture, then laughter is the
fruit you harvest. It's a sure indication that things are going well,
because before you can laugh together, you first have to learn to
communicate. The opposite is also true. When the laughter stops or
you stop laughing together, it can be a sign of some breakdowns in
communication. When you stop laughing with each other and start
laughing at each other, it's a sign that something is wrong. When you
stop making jokes with your spouse and start making your spouse
the butt of your jokes, it's a sign that some deeper work and healing
need to happen.

When you stop laughing with each other and start laughing at each other, it's a sign that something is wrong.

That kind of humor is nothing more than scars masked as sarcasm.

Humor can be an amazing tool, but it can become a weapon that tears couples apart.

When the same joke that used to make you laugh stops being funny, it's typically a sign that there is a drift happening in your relationship. It may be a sign that one or both of you have put up a wall as a result of unaddressed hurt. You've moved from loving each other as husband and wife to living as roommates.

This is typically when petty annoyances start accumulating. Frustration builds, and while you may not be on the verge of divorce, you're probably on the verge of a blowup, as neither of you will be fulfilled by the empty cast society tells us is what we should settle for in marriage.

No one wants to be a stereotype. That social media video you think you relate to, that meme that made you smirk—they'll end up making you feel empty if you settle for society's equation for marriage.

A marriage absent any fun will be filled with frustration—and likely it will be failing.

Your marriage is not a meme.

We fell into that trap once. We are determined never to fall into it again, and we are on a mission to keep other couples from making the same mistakes we did. If you want to keep the passion in your marriage, you need to keep laughing together. But to do that you need to learn to listen to each other.

REAL TALK

Jimmy

I love to laugh! One of the things that drew me to Irene was how she shared that with me—how we could find joy together just making each other laugh. To this day we're the couple at the restaurant laughing so hard that others start to wonder what happened.

But it hasn't always been that way for us. Before we got to working on our relationship and figuring out our communication barriers, there were long periods of time when there was more loneliness than laughter. We could be in the same room having the same conversation but not really hearing each other. We were coexisting—surviving, but not thriving.

Communication barriers have a way of making you feel as if you're stuck in the rough golfing. You're still technically in the game, but it's more frustrating than fun.

I want you to know something—something I didn't back then: God has much more for your marriage.

He doesn't want you to just tolerate each other, he wants you to be in love with each other. He wants you to experience the same passionate, jealous love he demonstrated throughout Scripture—even in the hard or dry seasons of life. Romans 8:39 tells us that nothing can ever separate us from God's love. Zephaniah 3:15–17 assures us that not only is he close in the hard times, but he promises to turn those seasons into a party! Verse 17 says that God will sing over his people *"like a new husband"* (THE VOICE).

Joy is waiting on the other side of the breakthrough; that's a promise.

Irene

I've read countless articles on marriage. Recently I read an article about marriage trends and statistics in which the authors wrote about common "final straw" material that couples list as their reasons for divorce—and, honestly, the nosy side of me was intrigued! I wanted to know which "irreconcilable differences" ended most marriages. Interestingly, "lack of commitment" exceeded even infidelity on the list![1]

Statistics don't lie: your marriage is more likely to recover from an unfaithful partner than from a spouse unwilling to put in the work.

But perhaps even more mind-blowing was that not one single couple polled agreed with each other on what the final straw was. When asked separately, not one couple had given a matching answer. That hit me hard. Although every couple agreed they had an irreconcilable difference, none of them agreed on what the difference was.

If we're not communicating well in marriage, we may actually disagree on what we're even arguing about!

I sat back in my chair and thought about that. What does it mean to communicate well? There's a lot of listening involved in marriage, and sometimes it can feel a bit monotonous: How was your day, honey? Did you pick up the dry cleaning? Traffic was bad today . . . *Do you really have to be "present" for all of these conversations?*

I love history, and I study a lot of World War II history in particular. There are some fascinating communication blunders in this period but also some incredible successes. One has to do with code cracking. The thing about codes is that you have to know the source. The Nazi code was cracked with the discovery of the Enigma machine—as complicated as this device was, as soon as the Allied troops knew the source, the code was easily deciphered.

The United States Marines, however, took a different approach and recruited Navajo who spoke their indigenous, unwritten language to help them develop and communicate by secret code. Because there was no written source, enemy forces were at a complete loss as to how to crack this code. Tremendous victories were accomplished as a result of the Navajo Code Talkers' linguistic contribution.[2]

The opposite is accomplished in marriage. If we are unable to understand the source behind our spouse's communication style, it can be impossible to decipher what they're trying to say. And the statistics we just looked at show that marriages can end because two people couldn't navigate their differences—they never learned how to "crack the code" and, as a result, couldn't even agree on why they were divorcing.[3]

The inability to discuss our *differences* in communication will lead to *dysfunction* in our communication.

But there is work in deciphering a communication style, and usually a style is modeled after what a person has known or experienced. In my family the communication style modeled was mostly that you didn't communicate—that your voice didn't need to be heard or your feelings expressed. In Jimmy's family feelings were felt, heard, yelled— the style was loud in every sense of the word. This made deciphering our very different sources difficult. Whereas he would yell, I had a tendency to curl up in my closet and cry alone. Neither was helpful or constructive. Neither was getting us closer to cracking the code. So what should you do?

In a word: *listen.*

Let me ask you: Have you found yourself overwhelmed by the task of listening? Has it started to feel like a chore? Does it seem as if the everyday, mundane topics are suddenly all you're talking about with your spouse? Has boredom set in and you can start comparing your conversations to what you see on TV or in movies?

First off, the perfect marriage doesn't exist. Hollywood may try to convince us that it does, but that is only because "happily ever after" sells much better than "they worked really hard." Every marriage, no matter how healthy it is, is still between two humans—two imperfect people. Even when those two people are deeply in love, they are still going to get on each other's nerves. Everyone has annoying habits, and everyone has boring information that is nonetheless necessary to communicate throughout the normal course of a week: *we're out of milk, the child has a doctor's appointment on Tuesday, we need to change the AC filter,* and so on. None of this is sparkling conversation, but if not communicated, it could lead to an issue later.

Not only is mundane conversation sometimes necessary, but it can also help us decipher our spouse's code. The things that preoccupy us are often indicative of needs that weren't met in our childhoods.

Additionally, listening to the mundane is like making a deposit. When I ask Jimmy to clear the empty water glasses off his nightstand and I find them in the sink later, I feel heard. It was a silly annoyance, a small request in relation to the big picture, but when someone you love cares about something simply because you care about it, it builds trust. It shows that they are on your side; not only are you heard, but your concerns, no matter how small, are valuable simply because they concern you. And that deposit doesn't go unnoticed—trust accumulates and creates that safe place where your spouse can confide. The little things are a way to build toward the bigger things.

I like to think of it as a house. Picture your marriage as a building, with a foundation, walls, and a roof. The structure may be incredibly well built, but no matter how good of a shape it's in, it's not perfect. Every building has cracks that require some upkeep. The same is true for marriage. Even the strongest, most compatible couples will find some cracks along the way. It's not a matter of *if,* it's a matter of *when.*

So what do you look for? Here are three signs that you are experiencing cracks in your marriage:

1. You used to laugh together a lot, but now your relationship is absent any fun.
2. You stop being intentional about connecting—now you're withholding.
3. You tolerate the person you used to celebrate.

Can you relate to any of these? If yes, the good news is that cracks are relatively easy to fix. The bad news is that if unaddressed, cracks will keep getting bigger and can turn into real problems.

I once read an article about a couple who divorced over some dirty dishes. The article was written by the husband. He talked about his bad habit of leaving dirty dishes by the sink. His wife confronted him about it multiple times, doing her best to communicate how much it frustrated her, but he never changed his behavior. In the article he admitted how he never even tried to figure out why it bothered her so much.

He was shocked when she filed for divorce. Hindsight may have made their issues far more apparent, but at the time he couldn't see that they had a massive communication problem.

After some soul-searching, he had to be honest with himself: His wife had regularly communicated things she wanted him to address. She had made an effort to tell him the things that hurt her and tried to explain why certain things bothered her, but he didn't listen. The root of their issue was that he had been unwilling to do the work. He had been unwilling to listen when it concerned the seemingly little things and instead chalked it up to her being a nag.

Unfortunately, those little things added up. When he refused to listen to the "little" things, she didn't feel able to bring up the bigger things. The little cracks got bigger and bigger until their marriage fell apart. And, really, it wasn't about dishes. The source was her childhood, growing up not feeling acknowledged by her parents. She brought this wound into their marriage, but because her husband dismissed her concerns or requests, she felt like she had as a child—as though her opinions and thoughts didn't matter. The pain of that led her to distance herself from him. The idea of talking about it seemed pointless—if he wouldn't even listen when asked to rinse his dishes, why would she bring up something deeply personal? With no indication that deeper conversation was welcome or that they had any safe place to communicate, she continued to distance herself.

We all distance ourselves if we feel we are about to be rejected, and over time this instinctual reaction leads to a wall. In this case it led to a wall that was insurmountable. By the time he was willing to acknowledge his lack of effort, it was too late. Maybe a little empathy about a small concern could have avoided this outcome; after all, it wasn't about the dishes, it was about her not feeling seen or valued by her husband. What was masked as a simple chore was actually a major issue.

Remember the first statistic I mentioned? A marriage is more likely to recover from unfaithfulness than from a spouse's unwillingness to do the work. A good rule of thumb for a two-equals-one marriage: if it matters to your spouse, it should matter to you.

If it matters to your spouse, it should matter to you.

Certain things may feel small and insignificant to you, but the point of being together is that both opinions matter. You might disagree on the severity or importance of an issue, but the point of a partnership is that both people feel seen, loved, and cared for. Minimizing your spouse's reality, or acting in a way that makes your spouse feel the opposite of cared for, creates a crack in the foundation. If left unaddressed, even a small crack can threaten the integrity of a structure. Be careful not to minimize someone else's experience simply because you didn't have the same.

Know this: what your spouse cares about is yours to care for.

Communication is how we fix the cracks. Remember, as healing as laughter and good times can be, we have to be able to talk to each other before we can laugh together.

What your spouse cares about is yours to care for.

TWO-EQUALS-ONE CHALLENGE

Write down a concern or request your spouse has made recently that you haven't followed up on. It doesn't have to be a major undertaking—like the dishes, this is a small gesture to make your spouse feel seen. Maybe it's closing cabinet drawers or not dropping off the dry cleaning. Whatever the gesture, make a point of getting it done for your spouse. If you can't think of anything, ask your spouse for a way that you can help them this week. Something specific.

PRAYER

Father, thank you for my spouse. My spouse is a gift you created uniquely on purpose. Help us to honor each other even in the mundane moments of life. Help us to be attentive to one another's needs and patient when we have differing expectations. In Jesus' name, amen.

CHAPTER SEVEN

THE TALE OF THE TIGER
AND THE TURTLE

Your communication styles radically affect
your ability to understand each other.

Communication may be the most challenging part of marriage. Listening is key, but we also need to be conscious of our delivery—the way in which we express ourselves. We are two different people who respond to things differently and express things in different ways; even our emotional responses will differ. It can be hard to navigate through all of that to connect to one another.

Do you ever feel as if your spouse speaks another language? Like some days you say "red" and they hear "blue"? It's hard not to read into it. We all want to be understood by our spouse, and miscommunications can go beyond making us feel disconnected—they can leave us feeling hurt or rejected. If this becomes a pattern, it can lead to feelings of hopelessness. We start to say things like

"My spouse doesn't understand me." And we start to believe they never will.

Does this sound familiar? Are you experiencing this in your marriage? Are conflicts difficult to resolve because one or both of you shut down, become passive-aggressive, or avoid conversations altogether because you know you will inevitably feel more stressed and disconnected? Maybe you're even wondering how two people with two different filters, backgrounds, and communication styles can ever get to a place where you aren't warring against each other.

That was our story.

For years we struggled to communicate, unable to heal wounds caused by miscommunication. By the time one conflict was resolved, we had discovered a new way to verbally injure one another. Our inability to communicate resulted in harmful words, a lack of attentiveness to each other's needs, and flat-out disconnection.

If you're like us, you've found yourself stuck in a painful cycle, one that leaves you feeling alone in your marriage and unloved by your spouse. You are undoubtedly struggling with a longing to be known, desired, and heard. Deep down, you want your spouse—more than anything—to open up to you. You want to be the one person with whom they share their most intimate thoughts, fears, and wounds.

This is what a two-equals-one marriage should be, but without that safe place in marriage, it is virtually impossible to have, because when we feel unheard by our spouse, we lose trust in our relationship. The question becomes this: *How do we get our relationship to the point where both of us feel safe enough to share matters of our hearts?*

It's taken us several years, and we've worked very hard at understanding our communication styles, but it has radically changed our ability to understand one another and restored a true sense of safety— where we feel as though we can talk to each other about anything. In all our work on communication, we found the most important factor was how we listen. Listening is more than simply hearing the words our spouse is saying.

At the beginning of our journey, we thought of communication as the sharing of information and, in terms of what to work on, perhaps expressing ourselves more clearly. We have found, however, that the way we receive information from our spouse is just as crucial to the health of our relationship, if not more.

The rest of part 2 will be full of helpful tips and techniques that will improve your and your spouse's ability to communicate, but none of these techniques will help you and your spouse unless you first identify your communication styles. For us, a pivotal part of our journey was the tale of the tiger and the turtle.

> **In all our work on communication, we found the most important factor was how we listen.**

REAL TALK

Irene

There have been a lot of suggestions made in counseling that surprised us—techniques and concepts that seemed counterintuitive or downright silly until we tried them. We will never forget the day our counselor brought up the tiger and the turtle. We both looked confused, both thinking of the children's book *The Tortoise and the Hare*, shaking our heads, then finally asking for clarification.

It turns out these are descriptors for two very different communication styles. Jimmy is the tiger—the more assertive one in our marriage. Whenever communicating needs or wants, the tiger says it how it is. There's no pretense or need to sugarcoat. The tiger isn't averse to conflict and tends to be loud or demonstrative in a way that can seem exaggerated. When it comes to conflict, the tiger faces things head-on; no need to avoid them. In fact, avoidance is frustrating to the tiger. It feels like weakness or, at the very least, a delay of what is necessary. Tigers aren't good at toning down and can get irritated if their partners don't emote the way they do.

Jimmy's family was full of tigers. Whether with positive or negative emotion, the volume was high, and energy pulsated through the home. From an early age Jimmy was taught to say what he needed to say. It took years for him to realize that not everyone responds well to this communication style. And several more years to learn how to tone it down enough that it didn't make turtles run and hide.

Jimmy

Irene, if you haven't guessed, is the turtle. The turtle seeks the safety of its shell whenever feeling uncomfortable, stressed, or overwhelmed. Conflict is at the top of the list of reasons a turtle seeks its shell. Turtles avoid an argument at all costs because they never feel as if they're fast or strong enough to win the fight.

The turtle devotes all its strength to creating a hiding place. Whether it's fair or not, aggression is seen as an attempt to intimidate. This was Irene's example growing up. She watched her dad withdraw anytime her mom wanted to talk to him, not in a healthy way but out of avoidance. Instead of expressing his emotions, he would bottle them up and pretend they didn't exist. They of course did, but by the time he would express them, it was because they were too big to avoid, and therefore they would come out in unhealthy ways.

Many of us grew up without a healthy reference for disagreements— many of us have witnessed styles of communication that conflicted and were never resolved. If that's you, there is hope, and you can break that cycle, but you have to recognize your approach and how you express your needs.

YOUR TURN

Take a moment to consider your marriage. Are you the tiger or the turtle? How about your spouse? Do you have a marriage between two tigers? If that's your story, you're probably laughing as you read this. When two tigers get together, the sparks fly, which can be both good and bad. When things are going well, the relationship is easy and full of laughter. Arguments, however, tend to be frequent and extreme. Conflict usually involves raised voices and elevated tone. Tigers go at it!

Or maybe you're both turtles? It's common for two turtles to go a long time without a fight. This looks great on the surface, but more than likely there's a lot of undealt-with friction buried beneath. When two turtles are in relationship together, they must be very intentional about having difficult conversations and not avoiding issues—just because they're beneath the surface doesn't mean issues disappear. And tension can ultimately build to a breaking point.

But if you're like us, then one of you is a tiger and the other a turtle. When that's the case, it's important to identify and know our styles in order to effectively listen. Our marriage has been the tale of a tiger and a turtle learning to love and laugh together. It has not been easy and has required a lot of sacrifice, but we've learned how to love each other while staying true to ourselves. You can too!

We're going to take some time to individually address our communication styles and the lessons we've learned navigating them.

Jimmy's Tips for the Tiger

Before we go on, ask yourself this question: Do I want to be *right*, or do I want to be *understood*?

If it's the former, then read no further! Your natural disposition and communication style have more than equipped you to win all the arguments. If you want a healthy marriage, however, and you want to be understood, here are some tips for the tiger.

If you're a tiger who has married a turtle, you have your work cut out for you in terms of being understood. Being understood will require you to adapt your communication style so that your spouse doesn't feel the need to run and hide. What tigers need to understand is that turtles interpret aggression differently than they do. What the tiger would consider mild excitement, the turtle will see as an attack. The tiger has to learn how to empathize and filter its words, demeanor, and volume through the turtle's lens.

In the New Testament, the book of James has some great insight for tigers. The book itself is actually a letter, and in it, James says this: "My dear brothers and sisters, take note of this: Everyone should be quick to listen, slow to speak and slow to become angry" (v. 19). Those of us who are tigers often do the opposite. We tend to be slow to listen and quick to speak—and quick to take a tone or get angry. Learning to hear, and to be heard by, turtles means we have to tone things way down.

Even if you're paired with another tiger, your communication style will still need to account for your spouse. Ask yourself whether your tone is helping or unnecessarily escalating an argument. Are you more concerned with being right or with being understood? Because to function as a team, both people need to feel heard, and that can't happen if one or both are more concerned with being right.

Right about now, the tigers reading this are mad at me.

And the turtles are thinking, *It's about time someone said this!*

Remember, fellow tigers, that I'm writing this from my own experience. I've lived this, and I promise, it's worth the time and the sacrifice of your pride.

The next thing to recognize if you're married to a tiger is that acknowledgment is key. Because tigers typically know what they mean when they say it, it's important to let tigers know that they are heard and that their feelings matter.

Personally, I've had to realize that I need to give Irene space to process things out loud. When it comes to conflict, I often bottom-line things. Get straight to the point and take charge. I hold the entire situation in front of me and am quick to make a lot of high-level claims that shut down the rest of the conversation.

Meanwhile, Irene is a verbal processor. She wants and needs space to process all the intricacies. She wants me to give her space to do that, but as a tiger I often misinterpret her half-processed thoughts as truth claims, and when they feel like an attack against me, my natural reaction is to fight back with bottom-line ultimatums. Now, an attack was not her intention—she's just trying to gather all the information. That's me getting James's advice all wrong. That's me being quick to speak and slow to listen.

How about let's get even more practical—let's talk about body language. Tigers, your body posture matters. When you go into conversation with your spouse (especially if your spouse is a turtle), fix your face. Think to yourself, *What am I communicating with my face?* Are you smiling? Are you making eye contact? Are you scrolling through emails as your spouse tries to pour out his or her heart to you?

Psychologists tell us that over half of all communication is non-verbal.[1] Eye contact, facial expressions, even posture, says something. So what are you communicating with your spouse nonverbally?

Years ago in a counseling session, our therapist pointed out to me that my stature itself can be intimidating. Even when I don't mean to be imposing, my six-foot-three self, wearing my emotions on my sleeve, can be a lot for a petite turtle. I'm not at all ashamed of either of those things—in fact, I love them about myself, but I had to admit what the counselor was saying made perfect sense. I don't mean to be intimidating, but I am at times. So—and this might surprise you—whenever we're about to get into a difficult conversation, I lie down on the floor.

Why do I take the lower position? I do it because Irene's past in dealing with tigers would always cause her to go back into her shell. I now realize that whenever there is a concern, my posture should demonstrate that her concern is mine to care for.

When I take the lower position, I'm taking a position of humility; I'm taking a position to serve her and hear her rather than be heard over her. My being physically lower lowers my volume, lowers my pride, lowers my desire to be right. I want my wife to know that she is heard, that she is loved. And rather than becoming one of the tigers who contributed to her abuse, I am helping to redeem that trauma from a place of servanthood.

So when Irene wants to talk about something serious, I take the lower position.

Changing your *position* in the room is one of the most effective ways to change your *proposition*. Tigers, if you want to be right, take the power position in the room. But if you want to be understood, take a position of humility. Sometimes that's not easy! When Irene and I get into an argument and she starts saying mean or hurtful things, I get down on the floor to let her know that I am going to take what she said purposefully, not personally. I know that she says those things reactively—she is reacting to a tiger in a power position, so to combat that, I take the position of humility. It's disarming. And when we defuse rather than accelerate, we open the lines of communication again. We make being heard possible.

Changing your *position* in the room is one of the most effective ways to change your *proposition*.

Tigers can be intimidating, but they can also bring a ton of comfort. When you have the assurance that the tiger is with you, and will do anything for you, it makes the turtle feel safe and protected. Many marriages are trying to have the right conversation in the wrong way. Our concerns are justified, but we haven't done the hard (heart) work to make sure we are hearing and being heard by our spouse.

So I ask one more time: Do you want to be right, or do you want to be understood? If you want your spouse to hear you, practice taking the place of humility.

Irene's Tips for the Turtles

It's not just the tigers who have to make an effort; turtles have their own work to do as well. The first thing we turtles have to do is to get comfortable with being uncomfortable. Just because someone's reaction makes you uncomfortable doesn't necessarily mean it's wrong. Yes, it's the tiger's job to realize they're created differently than we are and to figure out how to lower themselves and posture themselves so as to be understood, but, likewise, we turtles must recognize our differences. We have to raise ourselves up to the best of our ability and not cower when it comes to confrontation.

The best way I have found to do this is to *change the connotation of confrontation* by finding the confidence to hang in it when I want to withdraw into my shell.

Jimmy is extremely caring and has a huge heart, but sometimes his thoughts slip off his tongue. Sometimes the impulse to say what he's thinking gets the better of him, and it can come across as harsh or critical. He doesn't intend it that way, but that's the tiger. For me, those are the moments when my instinct is to crawl into my shell. To shut down and withdraw from conversation to protect myself.

I used to put the blame on Jimmy, but with time I learned that my response wasn't healthy or constructive for our marriage. I had work to do.

My work (and the work for us turtles) was to identify when I was triggered. I had to recognize that often when I was tempted to head back into my shell, Jimmy was just trying to express himself. His reaction wasn't anger or aggression—which is how I had interpreted it—but just Jimmy being Jimmy. More than that, by hiding in my shell, I wasn't expressing myself. I wasn't communicating my feelings. I would stuff my feelings and maintain the artificial peace, but eventually the volcano would erupt. My internalized emotions would come spewing out in all the wrong ways.

If you're a turtle married to a turtle, this is likely the scene when you argue. Tension simmers like a pot on the stove and you both take turns securing the lid until eventually it reaches its peak and boils over. Fellow turtles, it doesn't have to be this way; we have a responsibility to express our feelings to each other before the mess.

Once I started hanging in the argument instead of withdrawing, I began to learn some practical ways to de-escalate conversations when necessary. The most helpful strategy I have learned is to simply acknowledge his feelings. Jimmy would often get loud because he didn't feel heard. When I would retreat, this felt like confirmation that he wasn't being heard. My absence in the argument was like proof that I didn't care. He would then usually get angry, shut down, say something like "never mind," and go silent. This left me feeling like an emotional hostage because nothing had been sorted out, so there was no clear indication of what I had done wrong. I would essentially tiptoe through the wreckage while he remained silent. Resentment built on both sides because he didn't feel acknowledged or seen, while I thought he was just being difficult and that he was impossible to satisfy.

I'll never forget the day I learned to name his emotions. Everything started to change! *If you are a turtle, practice letting the tiger know you see and understand how they are feeling.* When you are able to name their emotions and make it clear that you see how they feel, you will find a new level of communication, a deeper level of intimacy.

My final tip for turtles married to tigers is to reframe the way you see being married to a tiger. It may feel like a burden at times, but it's actually a huge blessing. I am weak in the areas that he is strong. Over the years Jimmy has helped me become significantly better at communicating because he encourages me to talk about the hard things rather than avoid them. He makes me better in my weak areas and vice versa. In other words, he pulls me out of my shell. I've grown in gratitude for his communication style because it has helped me become more assertive.

COMMUNICATION STYLES: STRENGTHS AND WEAKNESSES

Each communication style, whether you're a tiger or a turtle, has strengths and weaknesses. Things to leverage and things to let go of. To recognize these in yourself and your spouse, take a moment to consider the following chart.

If you're a tiger, ask yourself how you can use your natural emotive ability to help your spouse. The next time you feel a conversation getting heated, watch your posture and be sure to check your motives in everything you say.

If you're a turtle, ask yourself what your spouse is expressing and then practice making sure you verbalize the emotions he or she is trying to communicate. Challenge yourself not to check out when you feel a conversation is heading toward conflict.

TIGER: LEVERAGE	TIGER: LET GO	TURTLE: LEVERAGE	TURTLE: LET GO
• Safe and protective nature • Assertiveness • Emotive ability	• Need to win or be "right" • Adapt a posture of humility • Plans made without empathy for your partner	• Empathy: ability to name emotions • Desire for peace (without settling for artificial) • Care in verbalizing	• Fear of anger • Avoidance • Codependency

Up until this point we've talked mostly about verbal communication, but a large part of what we say is nonverbal. There are a few simple questions you can ask yourself to help you make sure your spouse feels heard.

The first question to ask is, "What is my face communicating?"

We've probably all been told at some point to "fix your face," and for the most part, at work or out in public, we're probably pretty good at maintaining decorum, but the truth is, sometimes we forget to do this around our spouse. If you want to put the work in and really learn how to listen to your spouse, your face is a great place to start. Can you manage your face? Can you make sure your face conveys how you're actually feeling?

Sometimes we're thinking but we're not communicating. Our facial expressions may be wordless, but they're communicating thoughts, feelings, resentments, fears, and frustrations. Your mouth may be closed, but your facial expression is not necessarily about what's coming out of your mouth, it's about what's going on in your heart. If your spouse is telling you something serious, is your face communicating that you understand the weight of what he or she is saying? If your spouse is telling you something sad, is your face conveying empathy? If it's something funny, does your expression convey amusement?

How about your eyes? Are you looking at your spouse or past them? Or worse—are you staring at your phone? Eye contact is one of the best ways to nonverbally communicate that you are with them. That *they* are the priority.

The trouble is that often our facial expressions can be confusing without our even knowing it. The French idiom *coup de grâce* translates to "stroke of grace" or "mercy blow." The trouble with translating this expression is that it sounds rather sweet in English, whereas in French it implies a fatal blow or a violent act. There is a seeming contradiction between the meaning of the phrase and how it gets interpreted. Sometimes this happens with our body language or facial expressions—we think we're conveying one thing, but what we emote has the opposite effect.

Don't be afraid to listen to what your spouse tells you in response to your expressions. Their feedback is invaluable in this process, as your spouse is the one person you're trying to better communicate with. You can even ask whether he or she thinks you're getting better at body language or if there's anything you can be working on for next time. We don't listen with just our ears; we listen with our entire selves. Start by doing the work to learn how to manage your face.

TWO-EQUALS-ONE CHALLENGE

Take a moment to think about this: Has your spouse been communicating something on a regular basis that seems small to you? Have you addressed it?

Today's challenge is to make it a priority to have a conversation about the issue. Without minimizing how he or she feels, enter your spouse's world and try to see the issue from your spouse's viewpoint by asking clarifying questions. Mirror back what you hear in response and ask if you got it right (more on that later). Once you understand the issue clearly, ask how you can help or what changes you can make to help resolve the situation.

It might sound something like this:

- "I noticed you've been cleaning a lot today, and I forgot to take my shoes off when I came home. Did I make you feel unseen? I'm going to be better about that."
- "You seemed tense when you came home, but I never asked about your day. I'm sorry if it seemed as if I didn't notice you. Is there anything you want to talk about?"
- "I noticed I left my drawers open again today. I'm sorry I keep forgetting—I know you mentioned that bothers you. I will do better."

Let your spouse respond, and hear them out. Resist the temptation to become defensive or to shut down when they express how they feel. The goal is to listen to understand—not simply to listen and have a ready response or solution for their feelings.

Any assurances made in this exercise will require follow-through. Doing these things will help your spouse feel acknowledged and cared for. When we address the "small" things our spouses care about, we honor them. In his letter to the Romans, Paul told us to "love one another with brotherly affection. Outdo one another in showing honor" (12:10 ESV). In other words, even if you don't think leaving dirty dishes in the sink is a big deal, cleaning them is an opportunity to show your spouse honor. These small behavior changes are simple, unselfish ways to communicate love. They show that you're on the same team, that your spouse's feelings are important to you, that their perspective is valid, and that you care.

Is there something your spouse has shared repeatedly that you haven't addressed? Is it forming a crack between you and your spouse? If you can't think of something, ask them if you are missing anything.

Today's challenge is to address a thing that seems meaningless to you but that you know is meaningful to your spouse. The love between you will grow in an incredible way as you honor your spouse's needs and feelings. The tiger and the turtle can coexist!

PRAYER

Father, thank you for my spouse. Thank you for bringing my spouse into my life and giving me a teammate. Thank you for all the times we've laughed together over the years and for all the funny moments you've given us together. Please remind my spouse and me that you didn't make any mistakes when you created us. You knit us together in our mothers' wombs and love us each exactly as we are. God, teach me how to have more grace for the ways we see the world differently. In Jesus' name, amen.

CHAPTER EIGHT

I'M IN MY FEELINGS

The goal is not to think alike but
rather to think together!

Normally, we tend to avoid generalizing statements, but here's a universal truth: no one likes to be told how they're feeling.

Have you ever had someone try to tell you what they think you're feeling? It's downright frustrating, isn't it? The reason it feels intrusive is that your feelings are your own. Only God knows what's in another person's heart. Proverbs 16:2 tells us, "Motives are weighed by the LORD." We see the outward; only God can see the inward.

But this means you have a responsibility to communicate how you're feeling to other people, especially to your spouse. Your spouse can't know how you're feeling until you communicate it.

This is where many marriages break down. While on one hand no one likes when the other assumes how they're feeling or why they're feeling that way, if neither spouse expresses how they are feeling, they will be in a stalemate. And it's usually a stalemate that ends in tension.

Emotional health is the only way to win. Because you won't be able to communicate with your spouse until you can first understand your own emotions.

REAL TALK

Jimmy

I set the tone. My outbursts and general expressiveness set the tone in our home. This isn't a men-versus-women thing either. Generally, the person who is most vocal sets the tone, and when unchecked, that can lead to an unhealthy home environment.

Now, let me be clear, emotions are not bad. I think particularly some men need to hear this: emotions are a *good* thing. They're a gift from God. If you grew up hearing that tears are bad, I'm afraid you got some bad advice! Just check out King David in the Bible; in my opinion, he was the greatest king Israel ever knew. The prophet Samuel referred to him as "a man after [God's] own heart" (1 Samuel 13:14). Known as a mighty warrior, David fought lions and bears with his bare hands! A man's man.

But the man was in touch with his emotions. Look at what he says in Psalm 6:6: "I am worn out from my groaning. All night long I flood my bed with weeping and drench my couch with tears."

This isn't "my eyes got a little misty." He doesn't say "it's just allergies." No, this is an unedited and raw expression of his inward feelings. And David talks about his feelings a lot—he even talks about why expressing them is important. In Psalm 39, verse 2, he says, "So I remained utterly silent, not even saying anything good. *But my anguish increased*" (emphasis added). David was essentially saying: bottling it up doesn't work.

But if emotional outbursts are harmful and bottled-up emotions are likewise harmful, when are emotions *helpful*?

Think of it like this: Emotions are like a check-engine light. They come up when it's inconvenient (nobody wants that light to come on), and we generally want to ignore them, but they tell us that something inside needs to be healed. Emotions indicate something deeper that shouldn't be ignored, and you'll never be able to connect on a deeper level with your spouse until you first connect with yourself. So let's talk about how to get emotionally healthy.

Emotions are meant to be managed. But to manage something, you have to be knowledgeable about it. You can't inform others about a subject you know nothing about. We've all heard of IQ (intelligence quotient). Everyone had one of those kids in their elementary school, the kid who had a higher IQ than the rest of us. But did you know that EQ (emotional quotient) is a real thing too? Throughout life we have the opportunity to increase our knowledge and become more intellectually intelligent. The same thing is true of our EQ: We can learn and grow and become more emotionally intelligent. It's the essential first step in managing your emotions.

Your feelings are trying to tell you something: Emotional intelligence is the ability to tap in and listen to what they have to say. We must understand what's happening inside us so we can communicate that externally and build a healthy marriage. Now, sometimes, especially in the heat of the moment, that's easier said than done. Being emotionally healthy means that when you feel a certain way in response to your spouse, you recognize that he or she is simply revealing feelings that were already there. Your spouse is essentially a mirror

> **We must understand what's happening inside us so we can communicate that externally and build a healthy marriage.**

in those moments, reflecting the emotions you are feeling back to you—making them visible to you.

This can be a little difficult to grasp, so let me give you an example. Say I'm driving down the highway and I'm heated because Irene said something on the phone before we hung up that I didn't like and now I'm driving a little on edge. I'm caught up in the roar of the engine, maybe I've got some road rage going on . . . I'm weaving a bit, speeding more than usual, or ignoring other drivers I would otherwise be courteous toward. I could spend the rest of the drive ruminating on what Irene said.

Or I could reframe it.

What if Irene's comment didn't actually "make" me angry? What if she was only holding up a mirror? What if all these feelings I now am directing at Irene are simply a reflection in the mirror she was holding up to me? When I consider this, it gives me an opportunity to examine my junk—to collect my stuff and process my emotions before I respond from a place of hurt that has nothing to do with my wife.

The reality is, I'm in that car by myself. If an officer pulls me over, I'm not going to tell him that I'm speeding because my wife made me, am I? No. I am in charge of that vehicle in the same way I should be in charge of my emotions.

Here's the thing—your past *will* show up in your present. You will get angry at your spouse for things that aren't totally your spouse's fault. That's part of being in a committed relationship. Eventually you will disagree. Eventually you will fight. And Irene and I have been in enough arguments to know that it's hard to identify at times that your past has entered the conversation until it's too late and you've said things you wish you could take back.

Your past *will* show up in your present.

It's easier to curse and it's easier to shut down or do

something passive-aggressive than to communicate clearly. As a tiger it's always easier for me in the moment to lash out because communication takes hard work. It takes the ability to manage my emotions, quickly assess what's coming up, and respond to the moment rather than react in the moment.

This understanding can actually eliminate many arguments. When we own our emotions and properly manage them, we can help our spouse to navigate them as well. It's the starting point of getting emotionally healthy, and it can dramatically shift the trajectory of a marriage. When you take ownership of your emotions, you stop projecting your feelings or shifting blame onto your spouse, and it becomes easy to come together and help each other through your personal battles. You might be surprised, but the result is a greater level of intimacy.

It's not an easy shift to make; it takes a lot of practice (more on that later), but when you start to get it, the result is a lot less fighting and a lot more laughter.

Irene

I grew up with a "no talk" rule. There was only one person in our home allowed to express feelings, and that person typically expressed them in excess. I was taught, whether it was said out loud or insinuated, that crying was a sign of weakness and that if something was going on, keep it to yourself. *Bottle it up. Stuff it down deep.* I became really good at numbing my emotions, at pretending. When the discomfort became too great, I turned to alcohol to help. What I didn't realize then was that by self-medicating I was compounding our existing communication problem. Numbing my emotions wasn't fixing anything, and, in fact, I was making the problem worse.

I remember being in Hawaii and looking at the mountain. Steam was steadily pouring out of the top because, although the lava is deep beneath the surface, the volcano is still active. Eventually the mountain will erupt again. It's not *if*, it's *when*. And all that lava will come pouring out destructively and violently.

This is what most often happens when we bury our emotions. We hide them beneath the surface and may let out a little steam every now and then, but for the most part we pretend all is well. We are strong like the mountain—and just as impenetrable. This means that although we may appear to have it together, we are actually holding our spouse at a distance. We may even be telling ourselves that we're holding it in to protect them, but the problem is that those emotions are still there. We still carry all of those wounds, and they haven't ever been able to heal. Eventually the pain becomes too much, and we erupt. And, most likely, it will leave a damage path.

It doesn't have to be this way. It took me years to learn this lesson, but emotions aren't bad, and we were created to feel them. They exist for a reason. God's original intent wasn't for us to avoid them but rather to move through them. Jesus himself modeled emotions and allowed himself to weep, feel anger, express love—the Gospels (firsthand eyewitness accounts) record him expressing a full array of emotions (Matthew 14:13, 17:17, 26:38; Luke 23:34; John 2:15, 4:6, 11:35). *This should assure us that emotions are good!*

Over the years, Jimmy and I have observed through the couples we've counseled that the best way to keep the spark alive, to continue growing in connection, and to continue laughing together is to figure out your own emotions. *Knowing your emotions can strengthen your devotion.* Being able to name your emotions and communicate them to your spouse so they can understand how you're feeling is crucial because our words are framed by our emotions. Until we become fully aware of our own feelings, we can't help our spouse navigate them.

I love to ski. I've had the privilege of skiing some of the most prestigious slopes in the world. But there are a number of factors that come into play when you ski: you need the proper gear, the proper stance (how far you lean and how far apart your feet are), you have to be brave in going fast because going too slow will have you sinking in the snow . . . which brings to mind the weather conditions, which determine even further criteria that are important to running a course. But every skier knows that once these factors are addressed, there's a rush like you've never felt! There's simultaneously freedom and connection—you become one with the slopes.

This is how it should be in marriage: a freedom to express yourself and a connection to your spouse as a result.

That's a two-equals-one marriage. Leaning into your emotions is like a skier anticipating a turn—you have to recognize it and call it out. It's the only way your spouse can make adjustments and care for you. And it's the only way you can manage your own responses to ensure that your emotions don't lead to more pain or misunderstanding.

TAKING RESPONSIBILITY FOR YOUR EMOTIONAL HEALTH

Emotional health is the only way to win because you won't be able to communicate with your spouse until you can first understand your own emotions. You weren't born with emotional health. Babies aren't born with the ability to regulate their emotions—they simply cry to express when something is wrong. In someone who is only six months old, this is endearing because they're expressing their need for their parents, but in someone who is sixty years old, crying when they don't get what they want is anything but endearing. This is especially important in a marriage, and checking in with your spouse is essential for the relationship.

Eventually, if you don't check in with your spouse, you check out. But before we get there, we first have to be able to check in with ourselves.

Sometimes a couple will come to us and spend the entire session discussing what the other is doing wrong. We see this especially in newlyweds; they go into marriage thinking they'll be able to "tweak" certain things about their spouse and then end up frustrated when the changes don't happen.

The truth is, you can't change other people. What you can do is take responsibility for your own emotions. When you feel yourself triggered by something your spouse said or did, it's natural to want to project that anger outward and argue. We often impulsively ask questions like "Why are you yelling at me?" or "Why are you making me so upset?"

> **You can't change other people. What you can do is take responsibility for your own emotions.**

These are natural responses, but what if, instead, we learned to look inward? Remember that no one can make you feel a certain way; the reality here is that something triggered an internal emotion. If you want to grow your emotional health, you have to get good at taking an internal inventory of what all is happening. Instead of directing your anger toward an external source, you must take responsibility for your emotional response and ask yourself questions about what that emotion is trying to tell you.

Why did I react like that?
Where is this feeling coming from?
Why do I take that so personally?
Why do I feel as if my identity is on the line here?

Consider Paul's advice to "take every thought captive" (2 Corinthians 10:5 ESV). You might wonder, why not just get rid of the negative thoughts altogether? But a negative thought or feeling has an origin—it came from somewhere. In war you take captives by making your enemies prisoners of war. Although I wouldn't say that emotions are the enemy, you do have to make your emotions answerable or they will attack you—you have to interrogate them. If you never figure out where your negative feelings or thoughts come from or why you're being triggered, you can never truly rule over them.

FIVE COMPONENTS OF EMOTIONAL HEALTH

Being emotionally intelligent is about spending time looking inward rather than outward. It means you've learned to govern your emotions by knowing, naming, and understanding the five components of emotional health. Let's look at those five now.

Component 1: Review

How do you see yourself? We all have plenty of opinions about those around us, but what's your opinion of yourself? How is your self-esteem? Take a moment to consider how you view yourself.

If you've spent much time in church, you've heard Matthew 22:39: "Love your neighbor as yourself." We all get a little convicted thinking about the last time we actually talked to or even said hi to our neighbor, and that's part of it . . . but did you catch the last part of the verse? Jesus isn't promoting narcissism, but he does say to "love your neighbor *as yourself*" (emphasis added).

One of the reasons we've found that people avoid checking in on themselves is that they aren't doing very well at loving themselves or seeing enough value in themselves. Do you love yourself? Do you own the fact that self-esteem is a continuum? We aren't always going to be on a mountaintop; we're going to have ups and downs, but part of being emotionally healthy is self-care. The thing about self-care is that you have to recognize your own worth before you care. Self-care involves physical, emotional, and spiritual health. And self-perception is vital for all three.

You will most certainly struggle perceiving and understanding what your partner is feeling if you can't perceive what you yourself are feeling. Are you in tune with your own body? Are you able to perceive what you're feeling?

Component 2: Reveal

Self-expression is our ability to reveal our feelings both verbally and nonverbally. Are you able to ask for what you need and want? For people who struggle with codependency, this can be quite difficult. It can feel very hard to ask for what you need, much less what you want. For many who struggle with codependency, this traces back to childhood, when you weren't allowed to express such things.

This can lead to a sense of needless, wantless denying of self, which leads to feelings of resentment toward others who aren't miserable. Irene's childhood was definitely formative in her developing codependent behavior. For our marriage this brought with it some complicated communication issues. Whereas Jimmy had self-expression on lock, this initially only led to deep feelings of resentment for Irene. And the brutal honesty that Jimmy prided himself on could at times be a weapon. Our fights became toxic because we were both so far off in terms of our own individual emotional health.

When you and your spouse learn to express how you're really feeling, it will change how you communicate. You'll notice this especially in disagreements. In our early years the smallest thing could turn into a huge fight. Now that we've grown in our ability to communicate our feelings, we can disagree without escalation.

We were at a restaurant a few years ago with another couple when the subject of fitness came up. That's when Jimmy made an announcement.

"I did it—I ordered myself a Peloton."

Hearing of this for the first time, in mixed company, I (Irene) swiveled in my chair. "You did what now?"

"It's nice . . ."

"I'm sure. How is this the first I'm hearing of it?"

"Well, you don't call me when you're going to buy makeup."

"You're really going to compare a Peloton to makeup?" I responded, eyebrows raised. "The makeup is in our budget—the Peloton is not."

"Well, I think it's time to change the budget."

We went back and forth a few times as the other couple awkwardly side-eyed one another. A few minutes into our conversation, the husband on the other side of the table texted Jimmy, "Are you guys arguing right now?"

"No," Jimmy texted back, and we both laughed out loud and decided to pencil that discussion in for a later time. The point of the story is that it was genuinely not an argument; we were both just expressing how we felt, and we know each other well enough now that it doesn't have to escalate. We can disagree without it becoming a fight. (And in case you were wondering, the investment was determined worthy after Irene started seeing the results!)

One of the biggest gifts of emotional intelligence and getting proficient at self-expression is that every molehill doesn't have to become a mountain. You have to do the individual work first, but then as you're able to spend time getting to know each other and experiencing life together, you get to a place where you can disagree without dividing. You can talk through disagreements without every difference of opinion becoming an argument.

Remember, the goal isn't to think alike but to think together. Emotional intelligence allows both of you to express yourselves with honesty and dignity. Instead of dividing you or demeaning your feelings, these discussions will actually draw you closer because as a result you will better know your spouse.

Component 3: Relate

Oftentimes interpersonal skills are underrated. Empathy is important in developing emotional intelligence and will make or break a relationship. Empathy is essentially your ability to appreciate or relate to someone else's feelings. It's about whether you are communicating your understanding of their feelings and behaving in a way that respects them.

Empathy was huge for us. You might be great at expressing your own feelings, but how are you at relating to someone else's? Learning to express empathy was a major breakthrough for our relationship. It's so important to not assume what your spouse is feeling or even that they know you care. Communicate what your spouse says, the way you understood it, to let them know you're really listening. This is extremely useful when you need to de-escalate a situation. By repeating back what someone said, and acknowledging or relating to their feeling, you can defuse a conflict before it gets out of hand.

Component 4: Resolve

Have you ever been in a room with a bunch of grown adults who are struggling to make a decision? We've all experienced that moment when four people are trying to pick a place to go for lunch, but no one wants to be the one to step up and make the choice. When you're the decision-maker, the burden is on your shoulders! If you pick a restaurant and someone gets food poisoning or the service is bad, you are the one everyone will point the finger at.

If you aren't emotionally healthy enough to handle that criticism, you'll find yourself running away from the decisions. But when you find yourself growing in emotional intelligence, you'll stop putting so much stock in critique. As a result, you'll stop putting off every decision in an attempt to avoid criticism. Instead, you'll learn how to make quick, informed, and wise decisions. You will develop resolve.

Component 5: Reframe

Stress management is about your ability to cope with stress and problem solve. It also involves your flexibility and how adaptable you are to change and transition. Change is going to come in life whether you would like it to or not. Transition can be stressful, even if it is for a good reason, such as having a baby or getting married. These types of life events are positive, yet the transition brings stress.

Take a look at the top five stressors, according to most recognized journals of psychological medicine:

1. Death of a spouse
2. Divorce
3. Marital separation
4. Death of a close family member
5. Personal injury or illness[1]

In our marriage journey we were often experiencing more than one of the top five stressors all at once with no skills to navigate those seasons. Lack of awareness on how to cope, empathize, have grace, or shift expectations led to arguments, misery, and resentment. We lacked the ability to reframe the stress we were experiencing, and the effects were toxic to our relationship. And according to the Holmes and Rahe stress scale (a typical reference that medical professionals use), stress doesn't just take a toll on your relationships—it can directly affect your physical health. The higher your stress score on this scale, the likelier you are to develop a serious medical issue.

How we handle stress can be either a positive or a negative factor in our lives and relationships. Emotionally healthy people know how to check in on their optimism levels, and they know how to reframe their stressful situations.

TWO-EQUALS-ONE CHALLENGE

Today's challenge is to do an emotional self-check. Be as honest as possible when answering these questions. You may be tempted to gloss over one or more touchpoints—don't. You'll never be able to fully express your needs to your spouse until you're willing to admit them to yourself.

Ask yourself the following questions:

1. **Review:** What is my self-perception? How would I evaluate the way that I see myself?
2. **Reveal:** Am I comfortable expressing myself? Why or why not?
3. **Relate:** How well am I able to empathize with my spouse? Do I feel compassion for my spouse's emotions?
4. **Resolve:** Am I comfortable making decisions, or do I feel the weight of others' criticism? Do I let my spouse's opinions sway my decisions?
5. **Reframe:** How am I handling stress right now?

PRAYER

Father, thank you for my spouse. I want to be better able to articulate my needs, so please grant me discernment as I work on my emotional health. We are committed to doing the work necessary in our marriage because we know your promise—we know that there is joy on the other side! In Jesus' name, amen.

CHAPTER NINE

STOP TAKING YOURSELF
SO SERIOUSLY

Seriously, stop taking yourself so seriously!

L ife comes at you fast. In the beginning of a relationship, it's easy
to get caught up in the romance—spending time together comes
easily. All you want to do is be together, go on dates, and talk. But
life has a tendency to get busy, and let's be honest, quality time is
usually about the first thing to go when the pace picks up.

When you first fall in love, you just want to lavish each other
with attention. But once you're married, real life tends to dull that
impulse; the day-to-day, mundane routine makes it all feel a bit less
magical.

We learned this lesson the hard way.

REAL TALK

Irene

About three years into our marriage, we were struggling. We had both left our corporate jobs in pursuit of full-time ministry, which led to massive lifestyle changes. And once we brought home our firstborn, it seemed we were always buying more food and diapers. In other words, we were broke.

But we also knew we needed a few days away for the sake of our marriage. We had noticed some problems communicating, and admittedly, as soon as the baby was born, my attention shifted drastically. Motherhood consumed me; I spent all my time thinking about and catering to our child, and our marriage took a back seat.

I knew this frustrated Jimmy because he would make jokes about it. If we had friends over to give him an audience, he would say things like "What do I need to do around here to get some attention? Put a diaper on?" That always got a laugh out of our company, but, deep down, it ate at me. I felt as though I wasn't enough. As if I was torn between being either a good mother or a good wife—I couldn't handle both.

Now that Jimmy and I have done the work, we can see what we couldn't then. I can see that Jimmy was trying to communicate how he felt, but he didn't have the courage to come out and say it, so he used humor or sarcasm. We can laugh at it now, but at the time I was too afraid to call him on it. Instead, I would shove my feelings down and then harbor a disproportionate amount of anger and bitterness toward him.

We were both insecure; it just came out in different ways. Jimmy made jokes and I would get quiet and deflect my pain. Remember the turtle? This is the manifestation of that in all its unhealthy glory.

Instead of telling Jimmy how I felt, I hid my emotions and isolated. Jimmy and I both were completely deadlocked in our ignorance. This meant that instead of checking in and communicating how we felt in healthy ways, we would let the insecurities win and check out.

Whenever that happened, I would spiral. I would tell myself:

I'm a bad wife.
I'm a bad mother.
I'm not enough.
He's going to leave.

This was my reality—my belief system. But it wasn't true. The problem was that I had no way of checking this reality, of examining whether what I was believing was true.

Like I said, even though we were ignorant as to how to navigate our issues, we were aware that we needed to get away and reconnect. To invest a little into our relationship. So, despite the fact that we were living on a third of what we used to make and now had a toddler at home, we seized an opportunity that only God could have made possible. One thing we've noticed over the years is that when we recognize our needs and take the initiative for one another, God steps out on our behalf. This time it was in the form of a friend's condo in Myrtle Beach. They offered it to us for a week, for free!

We packed our bags, dropped off our daughter with the grandparents, and headed to the coast. Now, even though we were staying at the place for free, we were still on a very tight budget—I'm talking microwave dinners and certainly no fancy excursions! One day we found an alligator farm

When we recognize our needs and take the initiative for one another, God steps out on our behalf.

that had no admission fee. *Why not?* We pulled the car over and spent the entire afternoon exploring the park.

At one of the exhibits, there was a talking parrot who would repeat your words back to you. I watched Jimmy's eyes light up! He loves to make people laugh, and a talking parrot as a sidekick opened up a whole other realm of possibilities. Those of us there sat back and watched as my husband came up with stranger and stranger phrases for the parrot to repeat, which the bird did verbatim. I couldn't help soaking in the moment that reminded me of our dating life before marriage—Jimmy lighting up the social situations while I basked in each new experience.

Laughter truly is good medicine. It can remind you why you love someone so much even in a difficult season.

But the show wasn't over. After his performance Jimmy was a bit winded, so he walked over to a lone plastic chair next to the bird's exhibit, intending to sit down. You need to understand that

Laughter truly is good medicine.

Jimmy was a big boy at this point, so he eyed this flimsy white chair a bit suspiciously. We all watched anxiously as he gingerly lowered his three-hundred-plus-pound frame into this poorly made, sun-rotted lawn chair. Just as we all breathed a sigh of relief, there suddenly came a loud pop followed by a thud, announcing that the back of the chair had burst, causing Jimmy to tumble onto the deck surrounded by scraps of the former chair!

This moment could have caused either embarrassment or hilarity. Fortunately, none of us had to make that call—the parrot made it for us! The parrot covered his beak with his wings and began laughing out loud—literally cackling.

Before any of us could even check whether Jimmy was okay, we were all on the floor bursting in laughter at the scene. It was one of those gut-level, almost pee-your-pants types of laughter, with tears streaming down our faces. My abs hurt, I was laughing so hard. Jimmy was in tears on the floor with us—he thought it was the funniest thing he'd ever seen!

Sometimes you seriously have to stop taking yourself so seriously.

That day it was as if the laughter was washing away the walls that Jimmy and I had built up between us. It was as if it covered our insecurities, allowing us to reconnect. When we left for Myrtle Beach to work on our marriage, the last thing we expected was that a talking parrot with a sense of humor would teach us how to talk through our struggles and celebrate our strengths.

Jimmy

I may have just celebrated my fiftieth birthday and can claim to be half a century old, but in reality I'm a child.

I laugh at stupid things.

Childish pranks—things I got in trouble for as a kid, involving farts or burps—still make me laugh.

Some of you may side with Irene on whether my jokes are in fact humorous (that's a conversation for another day), but the reality is that in the past when we've gone through seasons when Irene or I withheld laughter or we refused to let down our guards, we might as well have withheld physical affection, too, because not being able to laugh together is just as much of a deprivation.

Our proximity in relationship is directly affected by our ability to let down our guards. Think about it: if I have a wall up, Irene can't get close to me. That's the point of a wall—to keep people out.

Now, whether or not my jokes are funny isn't the point—the point is that when you're guarded, you are by definition unable to be intimate. The very thing we think is protecting us is actually hindering us.

You might say, "Well, my spouse has a totally different sense of humor!"

So do Irene and I. That doesn't keep us from laughing together.

When you're in relationship with someone, usually it's not the joke that makes you withhold laughter; it's not what's being said that you don't find funny.

More likely, it's what's *not* being said.

In our marriage, when the laughter ran out, it was because we were busy running from our issues.

Have you ever run a marathon? Or simply gone for a long-distance run? I definitely haven't, but I know there are important breathing techniques runners use to regulate the oxygen distributed to their muscles. Otherwise, their muscles will cramp and prevent them from getting any farther.

If you watch professional sports, you will often see athletes wearing oxygen masks on the sidelines. This isn't always a result of serious injury. If our muscles are deprived of oxygen, they can't function the way they were designed to. In the same way, those walls that you think are protecting you may be depriving your relationship of oxygen.

But taking down our walls requires emotional health—it's not something our spouse can do for us. I can recognize when Irene is uptight just as easily as she can recognize my guard, but we can't fix one another's emotional health. That's why the seven steps to emotional health have become such an important part of our daily life.

SEVEN STEPS TO EMOTIONAL HEALTH

Let's take a look at the seven steps to emotional health. These steps are practical tools that everyone can use for self-examination. Although seven may seem like a long list, once you get comfortable using them, they will become second nature.

Step 1: Practice Observing How You Feel

The starting point for emotional health is getting really good at paying attention to yourself. It may sound a bit self-absorbed, but you have to get in the habit of observing yourself and how you feel. Before you assume it will be easy, please understand that it's going to take practice.

Over the course of life, we all have figured out ways to ignore, numb, and distract ourselves from our feelings. And this isn't just the case for those who have survived major traumas. It's human nature to avoid feeling pain, so instead of feeling our feelings, we search for ways to turn our backs on them. If you want to grow in emotional health, the first step is to get really good at taking note of what you are feeling.

Open a new note in your phone and name it "How am I feeling today?" Then set an alarm for every day at noon, and when it goes off, stop and ask yourself that question. Don't just fly through the exercise; take some time to be as descriptive as you can be. Notice how you are feeling, name the emotion, and write down why you think you're feeling that way. This may be a challenging exercise at first, especially for the more nuanced emotions, but the more you do this exercise, the easier it will become.

Step 2: Pay Attention to Your Behavior

The journey to emotional health is a long road, but there are a lot of helpful aids along the way. One of the most helpful allies is your behavior. Feelings drive behaviors, so the things you do are often an overflow of the emotions you feel. Which means you can reverse engineer that equation and pay attention to your behavior in order to understand your emotions, because the things you do will tell you an awful lot about what you need to know.

Don't ignore your behavior. Ignoring your behavior would be like having a bunch of helpful books on your bookshelf and never cracking any of them open. The information is there, but if you ignore it, you'll never benefit from it. Get in the habit of paying attention to what you are doing.

For example—have you stopped taking care of yourself physically? One of the clearest behavioral indicators that you need to address your emotional health is when you get negligent about your physical health. Have you stopped sleeping well? Are you getting some form of exercise? Are you eating well?

While we're at it, let's talk about impulse control. An impulse is an intense emotion that jumps onto the scene and tries to call the shots. Growing in emotional health means recognizing the impulse, naming it, and knowing where it came from but not letting it sit in the driver's seat. Are you able to say no to the unhealthy impulses you are feeling? When your behavior is taking charge, pay attention; it's a sign, an indicator. Like the check-engine light on your dashboard, it lets you know it's time to tune in with your emotions. Let your behaviors inform you about your emotional health.

Step 3: Begin Questioning Your Own Opinions

Do you have any opinions? Anything you feel strongly about? Since you are a human being, we're going to assume the answer is yes. We all have thoughts and opinions about the world. What's right? What's wrong? What would we fix if we were in charge?

But here's the better question: Do you ever question your own opinions? Do you ever ask where they came from or why you feel so strongly about them?

No one is right 100 percent of the time; pretending like you are the exception to that rule won't help you on the road to emotional health. Do you ever put your thoughts and ideas on trial? Or do you assume that you are always right? When you find yourself having a strong opinion or stance on something, take a moment and ask yourself why. Listen to a few people who disagree with you; keep an open mind and see if maybe they have something to teach you. Then allow yourself to honestly decide whether you believe you are right or wrong. Ask yourself honestly, *Is my opinion true?*

Do you remember the show *Who Wants to Be a Millionaire?* The one where the host would ask a contestant a trivia question, the lights would go down, the dramatic music would play, and the contestant would win money for every correct answer. On the show contestants were given three lifelines; the most helpful, or at least the most entertaining, was the "phone a friend." The contestant could call someone from their list and then get thirty seconds to ask the person for help with the question. A part of the emotional-health journey is getting in the habit of phoning a friend. When a situation arises and you feel your emotions heading strongly in a certain direction, phone a friend and let them tell you their thoughts about your opinion. Let them be a barometer. Take what they say into consideration as you assess your own opinion.

Step 4: Take Time to Celebrate the Positive

It's a lot easier to see negative things than it is to see the positive. It's human nature to skew negative, to hold on to the bad without seeing the good. Part of emotional health is becoming aware of that and choosing to celebrate the positive.

If you've ever watched *Saturday Night Live*, you've probably seen a character by the name of Debbie Downer—she's comically always skewing negative. Although this is entertaining on a late-night skit, it's not healthy in a relationship. Stop being a Debbie Downer! There are lots of things to celebrate in yourself and your spouse. Are you taking time to celebrate? In the early days of our marriage, this was us. It seemed as though we could always find something wrong. And it's not as though we didn't have good stuff going on; there were many amazing things happening in our lives worth celebrating. But let's be real, it's easier to ignore the positive and focus on the negative—it just is. If you want to be emotionally healthy, however, you have to make it a daily habit to celebrate the good.

Step 5: Don't Ignore the Negative

Number five may sound at first as if it contradicts number four, but that's not the case. We can celebrate the positive and still be aware of the negative. If all you're doing is pushing down the negative things in your life, it won't make them disappear. Instead, they will assuredly rise back to the surface in all sorts of ways.

Ignoring the negative just to keep the peace doesn't make you a peacekeeper. It'll actually have the opposite effect. Peace for the sake of peace turns into resentment and fear. If you want to grow in emotional health, you have to stop ignoring the bad. Positive things are worth celebrating, but the negative ones have lots to teach you. Don't ignore the negative things going on between you and your spouse.

One of the most common mistakes couples make is that they ignore anything that might lead to a fight. When you grow in emotional intelligence, you and your partner can learn to fight fair. Remember—the goal is not to think alike or the same, the goal is to think together. The way you share how you are feeling with your spouse is everything. It will lead you to either destiny or disaster.

Step 6: Take Lots of Deep Breaths

One of the most important things to remember is you don't have to (and shouldn't) respond to your spouse as soon as you feel something. In fact, that initial reaction probably isn't going to be putting your best foot forward. We usually end up wanting to take things back, things that we say when we're reacting instead of responding. In those instances, take a deep breath. Acknowledge that your words were too harsh.

It's okay to take a break. Call a time-out. Take a walk, go for a swim, take a shower, or do whatever you like to do to clear your mind. Take a deep breath. And then take a deep dive beneath the surface to see whether you can discover what your feelings are actually telling you.

This way, when you communicate how you are really feeling with your spouse, you invite your spouse into the journey.

Step 7: Start Again at Step 1

There's no such thing as a permanent transformation in your marriage. God's never done with you; there's always more. *So keep going!* Emotional health doesn't happen overnight; it's a lifelong journey. The final step is to never stop growing. Think about emotional health like physical health; no one ever finishes getting in shape. There's no level you can reach that allows you to just sit on the couch and eat junk food for the rest of your life. Getting in better physical shape is a daily decision. The same principle applies to emotional health. It's a job that is never finished, and thinking you've arrived is one of the most dangerous places you can be— so never stop! Keep repeating steps one through six over and over again.

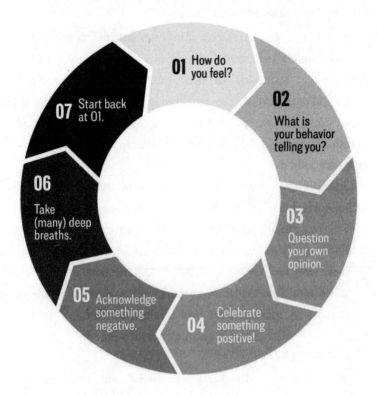

There's an ancient proverb that says, "The purposes of a person's heart are deep waters, but one who has insight draws them out" (Proverbs 20:5).

There is a reason we think how we think.

There is a reason we say what we say.

There is a reason we do what we do.

There is a deep well within each of us that drives our lives, but most of us aren't aware of it. We walk around on autopilot, without ever considering our actions or our motives. According to this proverb, one who has insight can draw meaning from these "deep waters." We need our partners to help us understand the *why* beneath our *what*.

Growing in emotional intelligence isn't solely about your own personal stability but also about your ability to draw out the deep water in your spouse's heart. When you know that the purpose is there and that you have the insight he or she needs, it is your responsibility to help. This is a mutual exchange, something that you both individually commit to as husband and wife. And when this exchange happens in an emotionally healthy way, you will find it tremendously healing.

Consider one more verse, because we were created for deeper intimacy, and having someone help you understand yourself is part of that design. Look at what the psalmist says: "Deep calls to deep in the roar of your waterfalls; all your waves and breakers have swept over me" (Psalm 42:7). The psalmist was writing from a place of pain, a place of hurt. But he identified great comfort in the fact that he was not alone, that "deep calls to deep."

When life hits hard, and it will, there is no greater comfort than someone walking through it with you. When your spouse is willing to meet you where you are, to walk with you through seasons of pain, there is an intimacy that grows as a result. A trust that bonds you together.

Are you emotionally healthy enough to draw deep water from your spouse's soul? Do you have enough emotional intelligence to help your spouse understand theirs?

Couples that learn how to do this will quickly find that no matter what else is going on in their lives, they have the ability to laugh together.

Remember: couples who laugh together stay together.

TWO-EQUALS-ONE CHALLENGE

Individually walk through steps one and two from the seven steps to emotional health. Ask yourself, *How do I feel?* Think through your emotions, then ask, *What is my behavior telling me?*

You might find that you're feeling anxious or sad. Maybe you're feeling hopeful or expectant. Whatever emotion you write down, consider what it's telling you.

Now that you both have answered questions one and two, it's time to talk through your responses. Remember that step three of the seven steps to emotional health is to question your opinion, and in this exercise the goal is to invite your spouse's input. We are not suggesting that you should tell your spouse what he or she feels (absolutely never advisable), but it can be helpful to consider each other's insights as to what your potential triggers may be.

Remember that as you discuss each other's emotional responses, your goal is to draw out the deep water. Think about behaviors you've observed that relate to your spouse's current emotion. What is the common denominator? Try to help your spouse trace the origin of this emotion and grow in emotional intelligence.

PRAYER

Father, thank you for my spouse. Thank you for the depth in my spouse's heart. Please give us the insight we need to help draw out one another's deep water—the purposes you've placed in each of us. We commit to honoring one another and take the responsibility of caring for our emotional health seriously. In Jesus' name, amen.

CHAPTER TEN

CHECK-INS

An incomplete journey through
your emotions will result in
incomplete joy in your marriage.

A big part of the two-equals-one marriage is the ability to laugh together. But you have to be able to listen before you can laugh. And in order to listen, you have to be emotionally healthy. That's going to require checking in with yourself and with your spouse.

Checking in is a life skill that we all require to experience joy in our relationships. The more you hone this skill, the healthier your relationship will become. Be thorough and take your time.

Getting emotionally healthy doesn't happen overnight. It's a process. And if we're being honest, you're not always going to feel like checking in with yourself. It will seem like a waste of time in the busy seasons, and at other times you'll want to brush it off as unnecessary.

But an incomplete journey through your emotions will result in incomplete joy in your marriage.

Remember how we talked about the importance of sharing secrets? Of sharing the things we struggle with? This is part of that; consistent check-ins are part of that process. There's work involved.

Checking in with your spouse is like working out; it's not always easy, and you won't always want to do it, but you will always feel much better once you do.

REAL TALK

Jimmy

For me, one of the best ways I've found to grow in emotional health is to check in with God every morning. Before you write me off for sounding like a pastor, hear me out: if I want to understand myself, I have to be in tune with the God who created me.

Here's the good news: It doesn't have to be anything extensive. I tend to struggle with any activity that requires me to pay attention for an extended period of time. I know, I'm a pastor, I should have long, detailed devotionals every morning. But my daily check-in with God generally isn't long. It is, however, consistent.

I pick up my phone in the morning, and before even checking my text messages or emails, I open the Bible app and read one short passage. Then I take a few minutes to pray, and before I go about my day, I take a moment to check in. I ask myself this series of questions:

- *What am I feeling today?*
- *Why am I feeling what I'm feeling?*
- *What's going on beneath the surface?*
- *God, what are you trying to show me or do in my life?*

Putting in the work requires effort, and at first it may feel a bit awkward, but you'll get better at seeing and acknowledging the way you are feeling.

Did you ever play basketball? The first time you learned how to dribble the basketball (bounce it on the court with one hand), it felt clumsy, didn't it? You had to get into a rhythm and get comfortable with the way the ball felt and moved. The more you practiced, the more natural the motion became until you could be running down the court without missing a stride.

Checking in on your emotions will start to feel natural as well. You'll find your stride, and when you do, you'll be able to help out your teammate as you become free to navigate your own feelings. I mentioned earlier how I love to be out and about and connecting with people. But sometimes, because I love it, I neglect rest in the process. It's taken a lot of check-ins for me to learn to realize when I'm tired. This is something I very much needed to recognize because when I'm tired, I'm more prone to do or say something that I will regret. I'm way more likely to snap at Irene over something silly. Or to just be on edge and irritable.

I'm not sure I've ever felt as tired as during the newborn phase of each of our children. Everyone warns you that, at best, you'll be sleeping for only a couple of hours at a time. It isn't till it happens, though, that you understand what that means. At best, you will be sleeping for only a couple of hours at a time. It's no wonder militia groups use sleep deprivation as an interrogation technique, because when you are sleep deprived, your filter isn't just weak—it's disabled!

These days our kids are grown, so my fatigue mostly comes from traveling, but it can nonetheless have the same effect. My family has a name for my tired alter ego: Jim. *Watch out for Jim!*

In all seriousness, it's in those situations when I pray something like "God, I'm tired today, which means I need to be on guard. Help me to have patience so that Irene doesn't think I'm mad at her."

Check in with yourself every day.

- What's coming up for you?
- How do you feel about your family?
- How do you feel about your children?
- How do you feel about your finances?

These regular check-ins with God are how you learn to take ownership of what you're doing. One sign that you need to check in with yourself is when you find yourself relying on your spouse to make you feel okay. Your spouse cannot

- make you feel secure,
- make you feel joy,
- make you feel happy, or
- make you feel peace.

Only the Holy Spirit can make you feel these things. Only God can do this for you. Hollywood wants us to believe otherwise—it wants you looking for the person who "completes" you. But if that's what you're looking for in your spouse, you will always be looking because your spouse can't fulfill that. Your spouse isn't there to fulfill you; your spouse is there to journey with you.

Being there for your spouse is a privilege, but in a two-equals-one marriage, you aren't reliant on your spouse or looking to him or her for your happiness. And considering the way seasons in life change, that's a very good thing!

Irene

As one who has struggled with codependency, I can honestly say it was difficult to get to a place where I didn't feel responsible for Jimmy's happiness. For the first eighteen years of our marriage, I lived on edge, feeling as though it was my job to regulate his mood.

I might as well have been attempting to ride a unicorn to the end of a rainbow.

It's impossible.

And, more importantly, it's not our assignment as a wife or a husband. It took me a while to realize that I was not designed to be the source of someone else's happiness—and this realization gives me joy to this day!

Now, I could give you scriptures such as Psalm 43:4, which says that God is the source of my joy, or Romans 15:13, which says that God is the source of my hope, but you might still be wondering, *Why are human beings disqualified—can't I bring others joy? Aren't we called to share our hope?* And the truth is that you can and should share your joy! But we are not the source. There is only one eternal source of joy; his name is Jesus.

You may recall how Jesus talked to a Samaritan woman at the well. He told her that he could give her "living water" (John 4:10). "It becomes a fresh, bubbling spring within them, giving them eternal life" (v. 14 NLT). Jesus was using a spiritual metaphor for something that would otherwise be a natural resource. Likewise, joy is not a natural resource, but we, as human beings, are. *We can't generate super-natural or spiritual things—they can only be given to us by God.*

If I want to come alongside Jimmy to encourage, love, and support him, I can't be the source of his joy. Only God can. But the beautiful thing is that, without the pressure of being his peace or his feeling of security, I'm better able to be there for him. When I'm not trying to carry a weight that is far too heavy, I am not burdened by things that are beyond my ability to control. I'm liberated to come alongside him, and my presence isn't obligatory, it's a choice. One that I freely make every day. And because I am drawing my hope, my peace, my joy from an eternal well and not from my husband, my source is never depleted.

Let's talk about practical ways in which we can support one another and what it looks like in real life when we apply this. Just as we individually check in on our own emotional health, we also make a point of checking in with each other. Jimmy and I have found that these check-ins can typically be categorized in three ways.

THREE LEVELS OF CHECK-INS

There are three levels of check-ins:

- Level 1: The Facts
- Level 2: Opinions and Ideas
- Level 3: The Depths

Let's walk through them one at a time.

Level 1: The Facts

The first level of check-in involves the objective though sometimes superficial facts about your spouse's day. What happened? Where did they go? Who were they with? What was the high? What was the low? Were they traveling all day in a stressful environment, or were they juggling the kids all day?

Every person needs a safe place to process his or her day. You can be that for your spouse. You can ask questions, sit back, and listen as your spouse word-vomits all the facts about the mundane. This is the easy part, but it's also really important. There's a reason that conversations tend to begin with small talk. We have to start slow, warm up, and get the facts down before we dive deeper. But at some point the goal is to move to the next level—from facts to the opinions and ideas.

Irene's Pro Tip for Level 1: Be Present

I've honestly struggled in this area: the basic, factual check-in. It seems simple, right? But the truth is that simplicity can be a stumbling block because it can seem unimportant. The factual check-in may not always be the most interesting, but it is the first step in creating a safe place. This means that your spouse should get your full, undivided attention. Let me be even clearer: no phones, people. Eye contact is crucial.

It also means that your face, attitude, and empathy should convey genuine interest in what your spouse is saying. Your posture and body language will indicate to your spouse that even the unglamorous and mundane aspects of life matter to you.

Maybe today he got stuck in traffic, maybe she got a good review at work, maybe he's simply telling you that the cost of gas stressed him out—whatever is on your spouse's mind, your job is to be present with no judgment or criticism.

It's that simple. It's not about your having the answers or solutions; you just need to be present.

Level 2: Opinions and Ideas

Once you give your spouse some space to tell you all about the things that happened, you'll probably have some opinions and ideas about what that means. For example, if she had a crazy day with the kids, you may have formed an opinion that she is exhausted and probably a little on edge. Instead of assuming that is true, however, your job is to find out if it's true. You do that by asking leading questions, then sitting back and listening.

Here are some good examples of leading questions to ask:

- "It sounds like you didn't have any time for yourself today. How are you feeling right now?"
- "I know you've had to travel all day, and it can take a toll on you. How are you doing?"
- "You have a big week coming up. I'm sure you're carrying a lot of weight on your shoulders. Is the pressure getting to you at all?"

Ask questions instead of jumping in and explaining how you assume your spouse is feeling. Repeat back what you hear your spouse saying in order to gain understanding or clarification; don't assume or tell your spouse how you think he or she should be feeling. Create a place for your spouse to verbalize feelings with no judgment, criticism, or response. This has to be a judgment-free zone.

Jimmy's Pro Tip for Level 2: Mirror

We've seen this term abused or misappropriated, but the term *mirroring* refers to a legitimate therapeutic technique. It's not about manipulating your memories or emotions; it's actually the opposite.[1] When you mirror what your spouse says, you are repeating back what you heard to ensure that you have the correct information.[2]

It's so easy to jump straight to your own opinions about what your spouse is really saying, but so much of the check-in is learning to listen—and by that we mean to truly listen. When mirroring, you are forced to take time to acknowledge what your spouse says before you move on in the conversation. It's more than a fact check;

this demonstrates in a very real way how intentional you are for your spouse.

Because repeating back to your spouse what you heard can sometimes feel like parroting, you can incorporate some of your own words in your reply, but try to be careful not to twist anything that your spouse said.

So, for example, if we are in the middle of a check-in and one of us is telling the other about a frustrating situation with a friend, the other will jump in and say, "What I hear you saying is that you're feeling frustrated with ___ because ____ said ____ to you. Did I get that right?"

Mirroring back what the other person says may feel awkward or even robotic, but it is one of the best ways to validate your spouse. It accomplishes two things: first, it shows your spouse that you are truly listening, and second, it allows your spouse to make sure that you heard correctly. Ultimately, it helps you listen to understand rather than listen to respond, which will help your check-in move from level two to level three. When you get good at level-two questions, you and your spouse will naturally find yourselves heading into the level-three questions—the depths.

Level 3: The Depths

What's really going on in your spouse's heart? As Proverbs reminds us, there is deep water down there; your job is to use any insight you have to draw it out. You are trying to dive beneath the facts, the assumptions, and your ideas about how your spouse should be doing and get down to what is really going on.

The truth is, we all put up walls, a protective outer layer to keep people from seeing how we are really doing. Walls are great for medieval fortresses and wartime barricades, but they hinder relationships. Your job is to figure out how to navigate around your spouse's defensive walls and help your spouse communicate how he or she is really doing. Oftentimes, you'll know you've gotten to this level because some new emotions will rise to the surface.

Walls are great for medieval fortresses and wartime barricades, but they hinder relationships.

For example, if a particular topic always angers you and your spouse, but as you continually check in, you feel some grief rise to the surface, that's a good sign that it has become a level-three check-in.

Every check-in might not get to the third level. In fact, at first, most of them probably won't. Getting to the third level may take some repetition. You have to become a student of your spouse. You have to learn how they think, how they feel, and what they really mean beneath the words they are saying.

When it comes to check-ins, consistency is key. The first time you check in, you'll spend most of the time in level one, but as you keep going, you'll notice yourselves flying right through level one and spending all your time in levels two and three. And, best of all, you'll realize that the more time you spend having level-two and level-three check-ins, the easier it is to come together and laugh. *And couples who laugh together stay together!* Laughter helps you feel as if you're falling in love with each other all over again.

Irene's Pro Tip for Level 3: Make a Vulnerable Request

One of the best ways to get down into the depths is to make a vulnerable request. A vulnerable request is when you ask your spouse to help support you in a way that has historically been difficult for you to talk about. It's how you show them that you are trying to open up and let them into a place that you used to keep them out of.

For example, historically I have found it difficult to communicate about mental health. This was a challenge in our marriage for many years. I wanted to talk about it, but it was hard for me to communicate how I really felt. I would get nervous . . . afraid of feeling weak, or as though I were slowing down our marriage. And when I really thought about it, I was afraid he would jump to conclusions as soon as I brought it up. I needed a safe place to process how I was feeling.

I vividly remember the day I worked up the courage to talk about it. Biting my lip, I softly asked, "Can I make a vulnerable request?"

"Of course," Jimmy said, sitting down.

"I need to talk to you about my mental health, but I'm afraid you're going to jump in with solutions before I finish. Would you let me talk out loud for several minutes as I process everything I'm feeling?"

That vulnerable request changed our check-ins.

Jimmy is very different from me—he doesn't speak until he's ready. He processes in his head so that by the time the words leave his mouth, they're the finished product. He says what he means. I'm the complete opposite! I'm a verbal processor. When I start talking, I'm throwing out a bunch of half-baked ideas. I say what I'm thinking, and until Jimmy and I worked through our different communication styles, that seemed to be the point of conversations—*they allow us to work through our thoughts together, right?*

I think you can see how this would create tension in our check-ins! Jimmy would take everything I said literally, while I was simply processing information out loud. He would say things like "Say what you mean and mean what you say!"

As frustrating as this was for me, it was my responsibility to help him see that sometimes I just need space to think out loud. Neither style is right or wrong, but they are very different, and until we understood that about each other, our differences caused frustration—often leading us to check out of the check-in!

My vulnerable request helped us to learn so much more about each other. These days we have language for this frustration; when Jimmy tries to jump to a conclusion while I'm simply trying to process, we call it "bottom-lining." When I start to feel he's bottom-lining, I usually feel myself checking out. Instead of getting mad and letting my emotions take charge, I make a vulnerable request for him to hear me out. He's worked hard over the years to understand how our styles are different. He's learned to be patient and let me process before jumping in and sharing his thoughts and feelings . . . *and it has changed everything about our marriage.*

Vulnerable requests have also led to safe words (and no, I'm not talking about some *Fifty Shades of Grey*–type safe words). There have been times when we've been out in public and I was triggered by something someone said or did—maybe it caused me to flash back to a painful memory—and I needed help navigating past my emotions. So Jimmy and I came up with words that are like a code between the two of us. If one of us uses a code word, we have given each other specific ways to respond. Ways to help. These words are between just the two of us—they're our secret language, which is intimately known only to us.

Sometimes safe words are simpler than that, though. For instance, let's say that, whether serious or in jest, something Jimmy says evokes a more intense emotion. Instead of reacting, I will simply say "ouch" and he immediately knows that he's hurt my feelings. This gives him the option to address that emotion and apologize—it defuses what otherwise might blow up into an argument.

We wouldn't have gotten here if we hadn't committed to making vulnerable requests of each other. There's a reason vulnerability is so scary. It's a risk to let someone else into the deepest places of your soul. But if you want a two-equals-one marriage, you have to learn to trust each other enough to go there.

Remember: this won't happen overnight. There's no dry-aged steak on a McDonald's menu, and, likewise, there's no express version of a healthy marriage. It comes as the fruit of putting in the work together.

One conversation at a time.

One check-in at a time.

One vulnerable request at a time.

LEVEL 01: THE FACTS

LEVEL 02: OPINIONS & IDEAS

LEVEL 03: THE DEPTHS

TWO-EQUALS-ONE CHALLENGE

One attempt at checking in with your spouse will not fix everything, but consistent check-ins can go a long way! Today's challenge is to schedule a weekly check-in. Sit down with your spouse and decide on a thirty-minute window every week where you can talk about what you're going through.

In the days leading up to your scheduled check-in, keep a list of things you want to discuss. Be specific and thoughtful in what you

If you want a two-equals-one marriage, you have to learn to trust each other enough to go there.

include. Then choose your top three and use the steps we've discussed to check in.

The goal is for you to do some sort of check-in every day. But we've found it's also very helpful to have something on the calendar every week for the crucial conversations. During these weekly check-ins, don't hold back. Before the conversation take a moment to gather your thoughts. Check in with yourself and be honest about how you are feeling. Then go into the conversation determined to share those feelings authentically with your spouse, while using these tools to see if you can draw the deep water.

Every week doesn't have to look the same. Mix it up and have some fun with it! Go to different places, talk about different things, and even when the topics of conversation end up being heavy, find a way to keep the experience uplifting by always choosing to love each other.

PRAYER

Father, thank you for my spouse. I'm sorry for any way that I have drifted away or let the fire go out in our relationship. I ask now, in the name of Jesus, that you would relight the fire between us. Help us to check in with each other instead of checking out. Would you remind us of our love for each other, the love we felt for each other in the beginning? Thank you for giving each of us the patience to put up with the imperfections in the other. Please teach us how to do that more every day. I pray in Jesus' name, amen.

CHAPTER ELEVEN

TWO TRUTHS AND A LIE

The goal is not to stop fighting; the
goal is to learn how to fight fair.

L ife is hard enough, isn't it? Give yourself permission to laugh.
Obviously, you and your spouse want to make sure you're laughing *together*, but sometimes for that to be possible you need to
loosen up.

Oftentimes, the tension you feel is a result of a false mental script
you've been rehearsing. You're hung up on a lie that's worked you up
into a defensive posture. You can't relax, let alone laugh, when you're in
a defensive posture. Ever watched a boxing match? I guarantee you've
never seen a professional fighter laugh during a match. The same is
true when we're feeling attacked.

The thing about lies is that many times your spouse has nothing
to do with the false script you're following. Sure, he or she may inadvertently trigger you, and that's something to address, but other times
you need to take the initiative and check those lies—to examine where

that thought or that feeling came from and own whatever deception has you playing defense against your spouse.

We need to rewrite the script and stop rehearsing the lies.

REAL TALK

Jimmy

Irene and I get to travel all around the world and speak at marriage conferences. We love coming alongside couples, some of whom are really struggling, and helping them fall back in love and life together again. But when we're talking to couples, sometimes we hear a line that makes us cringe.

"Well, I bet you two never fight or have a disagreement, right?"

Nothing could be further from the truth! Irene and I have disagreements all the time. It's not as if since embarking on this two-equals-one journey we've never again disagreed on anything. The goal is not to stop fighting; the goal is to learn how to fight fair.

Irene and I have gained enough emotional intelligence to check in with each other, hear each other out, and have disagreements without letting them destroy the entire day. We know how to fight fast, forgive fast, and return to enjoying each other's presence. But that hasn't always come naturally to us. Over the years we've had to put in a lot of work to learn how to fight fair. We've had to learn how to stop sweeping our problems under the rug and instead check in. Even when, or maybe I should say especially when, that check-in involves conflict. Checking in with your spouse is laying the groundwork for fighting fair.

When we're doing coaching sessions with other couples, you can always tell which couple has some conflict between them, because they are hesitant to do any of the exercises with each other. That usually means that something happened and they haven't addressed it. As if there's an elephant in the room, but they've managed to put a curtain around it and ignore it. Checking in forces you to pull back the curtain.

I remember one day early in our marriage when we were really struggling. We had a counseling session on the calendar, but at the time we couldn't stand each other. We didn't even drive in the same car. It doesn't take a professional to know that when a couple shows up in separate cars for couples' counseling to work on their marriage, something is up. We rolled up at the same time, parked in opposite spots, and walked silently into the office.

Our counselor was a portrait of peace. She was calm, cool, and collected—the last thing I was in the mood for! I didn't want quiet—I wanted to argue.

"Thanks for coming in today," she said evenly. "Why don't you take the next five minutes and affirm each other."

"Excuse me? I'm sorry . . . what?" I wasn't even trying to hide my tone. I thought to myself, *I'm not paying you to talk nice to my wife—I'm paying you to fix her!*

There were plenty of things I wanted to say to Irene, but singing her praises was not on my list. For the past thirty minutes I had been cussing her out in my head during the car ride over. How did you go from cussing someone out to affirming them? I looked across the couch at my wife and knew her well enough to know she was asking herself the same question.

Affirmations aren't easy on a normal day when you're happy with each other, but when you're mad, they are nearly impossible. But we did it. We both took a deep breath, looked at each other, and through gritted teeth listed the things we loved about each other.

I'm not gonna lie, the first few felt forced for both of us, but sometimes the first step is to force it. You have to start saying it until you are believing it.

The first minute was rough.
The second minute was disingenuous.
The third minute was a little bit better.
The fourth minute was a little more genuine.
The fifth minute opened us up—it readied us.

That's the power of the check-in. Learning to check in with each other even when you don't want to changes everything. When everything in us wanted to check out, we found the strength to check in. We found the courage to get to that counselor's office and affirm each other.

Here's the most important lesson every person has to learn: *you cannot complain about a relationship that you refuse to work on.*

Checking in with your spouse is how to put in the work. It's a mutual decision to get your marriage into better shape. Just like training at the gym, it will require regular, intentional effort. No one hits the treadmill one time and is instantly ready for a marathon. You will always struggle to have a two-equals-one marriage if you don't learn how to do this consistently.

You cannot complain about a relationship that you refuse to work on.

But every check-in looks a little different. Some are funny, others are serious. Some are long, others are short. Some are impromptu, others are planned. Some are fun, some are tough. But if the two of you can get good at checking in with each other, you'll be able to persevere through life's most difficult moments.

This is the first step toward fighting fair. This is how you lay the groundwork.

Irene

One day I showed up to a counseling session hot. Normally it would take a considerable amount of time for me to open up and share, but this was one session where I came in ready to express my feelings. I could name the emotion, I could pinpoint exactly what was causing it, and it was clearly Jimmy's fault—he was provoking me, and this behavior needed to be addressed.

Now, some of you are going to immediately laugh and take Jimmy's side, but hear me out. My husband and his immature high school friends think passing gas is hilarious—especially when they can trap their spouses in a confined space with the offensive odor. They even have a name for it—they call it the Studebaker. These pranks were driving me crazy!

Our counselor listened patiently as I explained the situation in detail. There was no doubt in my mind she would immediately address Jimmy, but instead a faint smile crossed her lips, and looking directly at me, she said, "Irene, you need to loosen up."

I was shocked. I had come in with a singular response in mind, and that was certainly not it!

Then, as her words started to sink in, I felt a release. We had been working through so many deeply rooted, serious issues—so many heavy topics full of grief and pain. *Permission to laugh felt like a weight had been lifted.*

Not every check-in has to be an emotionally draining experience. Not every expression of emotion has to be heavy. Sometimes we need to take time to laugh. Part of pursuing emotional health and recognizing our strengths and weaknesses is being able to laugh. That can be laughing at a shared memory, laughing at something silly, sometimes even laughing at ourselves! In this case that is exactly what I needed to do. I needed to be able to laugh at myself—to find humor in a situation rather than frustration.

What I didn't realize until that day was that our difference (in this case, a different sense of humor) wasn't a dealbreaker. Did you ever play that game—dealbreaker? Where you come up with a hypothetical dealbreaker habit or scenario (usually completely ridiculous yet comical) involving a boyfriend or girlfriend and ask whether it would be a dealbreaker? You might say something like "She is everything you ever wanted, but she insists on using a fake accent whenever you introduce her to anyone." Or "He's your dream guy, but he starts humming every time you kiss him." And then whoever you're playing with has to decide whether it's a dealbreaker.

These scenarios are intentionally ridiculous—the point is to make each other laugh, and we readily see the humor in fiction. Reality is quite different, though; we often fail to see humor even when it's right in front of us. We opt for serious instead of silly—usually because we're caught up in a false script.

Remember how we said earlier that we need to stop rehearsing the lies? At this point in our marriage, I was still guilty of seeing Jimmy as against me. I found myself routinely going back to this mode of thinking, which made it hard to see humor in anything, but especially in jokes that involved me. I had to rewrite that script—I had to remind myself that Jimmy was *for* me and that although our comedic styles may be quite different, it wouldn't hurt me to "loosen up," as our counselor suggested. Proverbs 17:22 states that "a cheerful heart is good medicine." I needed to laugh with my husband, knowing that humor can be healing.

THE TRUTH SETS YOU FREE

Lies have a way of creeping into our subconscious. One of the reasons they are so dangerous is because they're not always obvious. On display at a museum in Washington, DC, is a tube of lipstick.[1] Sounds innocent enough, right? It's actually a replica of a tube carried by an undercover KGB spy. And it's not a tube of lipstick; it's a gun made to look like a tube of lipstick. It's a deadly weapon.

Scripture tells us, "Death and life are in the power of the tongue" (Proverbs 18:21 ESV). Just like the spy's weapon was cleverly disguised, so, too, are many of the lies we buy into. *Lies* are defined as words spoken with the "intent to deceive."[2]

Truth is vulnerable.

Honesty is exposed.

Lies are veiled—covered up.

It might seem as though that would make truth uncomfortable. And sometimes it is—but how many of you want to get naked with your spouse? I'm talking emotionally naked.

True intimacy requires vulnerability; it requires honesty.

It requires laying your true self bare before your spouse.

Here's the other truth about lies: We said they are covered up, and not only does that bind you, but eventually it will smother you.

You can't be covered up and be intimate.

You can't be free and be bound by lies.

If you want free, unhindered, passionate intimacy between you and your spouse, you have to start speaking truth over the lies. For yourself and for your spouse. Share your weaknesses so your spouse can come alongside you—you have to talk

True intimacy requires vulnerability; it requires honesty.

about the lies. It will bond you; it will strengthen you. And as you do, watch how much closer you grow together.

TWO-EQUALS-ONE CHALLENGE

For this challenge, let's play two truths and a lie . . . a modified version.

Take some time to sit down with your spouse to identify any lies that you have been believing. They may be in the form of old wounds, self-doubt, insecurities, or anxiety. List ways you doubt yourself or fears that creep up on you.

Write them down.

Now replace each lie with two truths. The first truth will be a scripture that refutes the lie, but the second truth will take the lie, that false thought, and turn it around to create an affirmation for yourself.

It will look something like this:

Lie: I am not enough.

God's truth: "For we are God's masterpiece. He has created us anew in Christ Jesus, so we can do the good things he planned for us long ago" (Ephesians 2:10 NLT).

My truth: God uniquely created me with purpose. He says I am enough.

Lie: I'm afraid I will fail.

God's truth: "For I can do everything through Christ, who gives me strength" (Philippians 4:13 NLT).

My truth: I don't rely on my strength but God's. I am more than capable.

Take some time to review each other's lies together. Take turns affirming each other and speaking truth over one another. Rebuke the lies. Those lies are holding you back, so speaking truth over one another is claiming victory for both of you!

PRAYER

Father, thank you for my spouse. We speak your truth over the lies that are trying to steal our joy. We take back the permission to laugh, knowing our joy comes from you. It is a gift, and we gladly receive it. In Jesus' name, amen.

A NOTE TO OUR READERS

You may be thinking, *This still doesn't feel like joy.* You might still be feeling hopeless.

The truth is, marriage is hard work, and working through difficulties in marriage can feel like a trial at times. We know this because we experienced it. But what we want to tell you is that on the other side of hard work and perseverance is joy!

Paul said this in Romans: "Endurance produces character, and character produces hope, and hope does not put us to shame" (5:4–5 ESV).

The world may be telling you that your situation is hopeless. Your friends, maybe even your family, are saying to give up, but hope comes through perseverance. We didn't know until we experienced it, but there is joy on the other side! I honestly can't believe how much joy we have found. Our marriage is living proof that hope doesn't put us to shame.

There are no shortcuts to joy. You can shortcut to the feeling of happiness, but it lasts only a moment and doesn't produce long-term strength. Settling for happy is like cheating on a test—you get a good grade now, but you didn't learn the material; down the road, whether it's for your job or a simple skill you need in life, when you need to know the material that was on the test, you have nothing to help you. Only perseverance can produce hope, and that hope exists because you are on your way to joy.

We want you to know that we are praying for you even as you read this. We pray the words of Paul in Romans 15:13: "I pray that God, the source of all hope, will infuse your lives with an abundance of joy" (THE VOICE).

Don't give up. There is an abundance of joy on the other side—if you persevere!

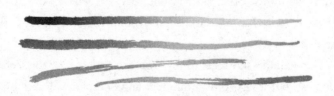

PART THREE

LONGEVITY

The pain of recovery is sometimes worse than the original injury. We don't say this to be discouraging, but it needs to be said. Dealing with wounds from the past can be harder than going through the initial trauma. The situation often gets worse before it gets better. You may even be feeling that as you read this.

Don't give up.

I (Jimmy) recently had an old basketball injury flare up. The initial knee injury was painful—I remember it well—but it was nothing compared to surgery. Sure, my knee hurt, but the pain was manageable. It wasn't debilitating. It was, however, holding me back.

You see, the injury had caused arthritis to develop in an otherwise healthy knee. If left untreated, I would never be able to attain the next level of fitness—I would have to stay in the "surviving" stage, never truly thriving.

This journey from 420 pounds to the best shape of my life has been incredibly challenging. It's tested me physically, emotionally, and mentally. I've worked too long and hard to get in shape to let some crunchy arthritis get in my way. So I had the surgery.

Managing the pain was thinking about the present, the immediate need.

Surgery was thinking about the future.

If you want a marriage that lasts, you have to be willing to dive beneath the surface. You can't avoid dealing with your issues. Avoidance is like taking painkillers when you know you need surgery. It'll numb you, but you will never reach the next level. Surgery means that you have to be willing to open some old wounds and allow your spouse into those broken places.

This section is all about the future—putting everything we've learned up to this point into practice so that you and your spouse can reach new levels of intimacy and growth. Nothing we've talked about so far has been easy, and this section is no different. I want to encourage you in this, however: as you apply these tools and principles, you will find a love that transcends anything you envisioned marriage to be when you were dating.

Life together doesn't have to be a chore. In fact, life together is what we were designed for. But we have to recognize the ways in which our past experiences and our personal modes of communication can cause friction or misunderstanding. Life is constantly changing, and so are we—if we don't learn how to grow together, we will grow apart.

One of the most dramatic changes we've experienced is having kids. Everything—good and bad—that you watched your parents do, you will likely find yourself repeating or desperately trying not to repeat. This can lead to tension between you and your spouse that you will have to learn to navigate for your marriage to last.

Longevity isn't about simply enduring; it's about creating a legacy that will last.

In the early centuries AD, Christians built carefully designed fortresses in the mountainous caverns of modern-day Turkey to escape persecution.[1] What began as the solution to an immediate need went deeper. And as it went deeper, it forecast their future.

These early believers made their homes tunneled into the rock face, and they created elaborate pathways through the cliffside. Some even designed military-style booby traps to ward off potential enemies. Today many of these passages have been turned into luxury homes and hotels.[2] Initially, these families hid in the caves to survive—to hide. But what they created went far beyond that.

Intricate artwork and detailed carvings are visible to this day—some nearly two thousand years old. Not only that, but the defensive systems they created within the cave homes speak to their ingenuity and craftsmanship. They weren't thinking only of the present. They were thinking of the future. And, as a result, what they built is still enjoyed today. They left a legacy because they were willing to do the hard work. They were willing to go deeper, to dig (literally) beneath the surface.

This section is all about action.

If you want your marriage to be more than a barren cave—if you want the enduring legacy that stands the test of time—now is when you break out the tools and get to work.

CHAPTER TWELVE

SAFE PLACE

Fight the feeling that fears are final.

Longevity requires navigating life's seasons together. The change of season from singlehood to married life requires you to be sensitive to the needs of your spouse. Some friends, along with some habits from your single days, will not make the transition with you.

This isn't about ditching everything from before you were married, but your spouse should take priority. This is true for each of you; if one of you has an issue, you both have an issue.

REAL TALK

Irene

I remember in our early years, as our church grew, it brought our lives into yet another transition. As our congregation expanded, so did our online presence. That can be a double-edged sword. I remember

Longevity requires navigating life's seasons together.

the day that Jimmy shared with me some messages he had been getting in his DMs from models. Let's just say these ladies were not respectful of the covenant of marriage!

Jimmy shared them with me, not to upset me, but for the purpose of transparency and accountability. Let's be clear: There is a world of people who are not going to respect your marriage. They are not going to care about violating trust or how hard you work to make your marriage last. We can't rely on the encouragement of others to champion our marriage, and, furthermore, we must arm ourselves against attacks.

One thing Jimmy and I have found helpful is the "couple bubble." It's something I read about in Stan Tatkin's book *Wired for Love*[1]— Jimmy and I call it our "safe place." See, what the models who thought they were slick sliding into my husband's DMs didn't know is that they were not welcome in the bubble. The bubble is an exclusive list: If you're not listed on our marriage certificate as husband or wife, you're not on the list. You're not in the bubble.

Ever been to a party or an event where you had to be "on the list"? The list exists for a number of reasons, but mainly because the event is meant for a certain group of people; it's how you keep it exclusive— you turn away those whose names aren't written down. Say what you will about snobby functions for the socially elite, but your marriage should be guarded even more exclusively.

Sometimes in marriage we can feel pressure to perform for everyone else. Suddenly we are barraged by opinions from his friends or her family or even what we see other people doing. We find ourselves letting other people we may not even know influence us and our behavior toward our spouse. To the point that even if we manage to schedule a date night, we feel as if it has to look a certain way—it has to be at a nice restaurant or an underground, unlisted concert . . . or we have to post about it on social media with just the right caption (otherwise, did it really even happen?).

Want to know my favorite date nights?

Jimmy all to myself + charcuterie board for dinner + movie on the couch.

When we have a date like this, we are free from interruptions. It's just the two of us. We pick dinner, we choose the movie—if there even is a movie. It's our choice, our bubble.

I'm not saying this is how everyone's date night will or should look, but this is my favorite. There was a time when this would've sounded lame—like we were a boring old couple. But as we began to do the work of marriage, the love between us grew to a place where I became jealous of my time with my husband. I stopped caring about what was the "cool" thing to do or what the current trend for a night out was and cared only that he and I got to call the shots together. That whatever our date night looked like, it was what we felt like doing.

As a result of the time investment, we have an index of inside jokes. We have no trouble turning away uninvited guests and protecting our couple bubble. Your couple bubble will look different from ours—it should. It should be about just the two of you. The choices you make shouldn't be about what anyone else thinks. Your friends' opinions, your followers on social media—that's all white noise.

But the couple bubble goes a step further than social situations— the bubble is also about improving your sex life. *Remember how I said the bubble is exclusive? How it builds trust?* Trust leads to honesty and vulnerability, and, friend, let me tell you, that kind of connection in marriage goes beyond simple mealtime conversation.

That kind of connection has as its fruit a greater future. In fact, that kind of connection is transformative because the pain from your past becomes the very thing that bonds you more passionately.

Even your deepest hurts don't have to hide in the bubble.

As a survivor of sexual abuse, I struggle at times to be present in the bedroom; flashbacks and triggers steal my focus. I used to fake it, but as you can imagine, this only led to mistrust. *This is an example of your past showing up in your present.* When Jimmy and I cultivated a safe place where I could share, I was able to tell him what I was dealing with and be honest.

This not only led to deeper intimacy but also helped him understand that I wasn't disconnecting because of him. Today we use safe words or safe phrases. For example, if I'm struggling, I ask Jimmy to "help me be present." Jimmy knows what that phrase means, and it helps us connect. He knows that my struggle has nothing to do with him or his actions, and the honesty only grows our intimacy.

You may be struggling or feeling broken in this area today. You might be frustrated or unsure how to express your needs to your spouse. I want to tell you that there is hope, and there is healing— you don't have to miss out on intimacy with your spouse because of your past trauma. But to have that level of intimacy, you must do the work to build trust.

Jimmy

Transitions are perhaps the hardest obstacle when it comes to longevity. Life comes in seasons, and transitioning through those seasons is rarely smooth. Transitions mark the end of a particular phase of life and the beginning of something new. Even positive transitions mark the end of something: when you get married, your singlehood is over; when you graduate, you're no longer a student; when you get that promotion, you move into a new role, which means you say goodbye to the old.

For many people, this is when insecurities creep in, and we tend to focus solely on what is ending. We fixate on the negative. And often we make our spouse the villain robbing us of what we previously enjoyed.

Irene and I struggled through many transitions. We villainized each other on countless occasions. There are an infinite number of reasons we do this, but at the root is a fear of not getting what we want.

The book of James has a lot to say about our wants and desires. In this letter James doesn't mince words. Some call him harsh, and maybe it's the tiger in me, but I find his directness refreshing! In chapter 4, he's actually talking about the way the churches are approaching prayer. You see, the believers were unhappy. They were playing comparison games and had begun to argue or sue others to get what they wanted. They were out of joy and desperately grabbing for temporary happiness. James says this: "You do not have because you have chosen not to ask. And when you do ask, you still do not get what you want because your motives are all wrong—because you continually focus on self-indulgence" (4:2–3 THE VOICE).

In other words, you will never be satisfied as long as you're focusing on yourself. If the way you are communicating (or not communicating) your needs to your spouse is motivated by self and is not about making an intentional investment in your marriage, it will at best produce temporary happiness. It will in no way benefit the longevity of your relationship.

With every transition your ability to care for your spouse will be tested. When Irene first got pregnant, we were ecstatic. I was going to be a dad; we were starting our family! But it didn't take long before the new baby meant a new phase of life had begun and the old one was gone. Any parent will tell you that kids can and do hijack your life—your entire schedule, your every plan, will have to take into consideration this tiny human. When you eat, let alone when you go on a date, even when you sleep will inevitably be affected by this little freeloader. There will be plenty of times you won't be getting what you want.

In this transition I villainized Irene. I saw her as withholding, as preferring the role of mother to the role of wife. Instead of coming alongside her in this season and seeing what she needed, instead of telling her how much I wanted time with her, I made petty jabs that in hindsight were nothing more than desperate grabs for attention. I wasn't thinking like a team, I wasn't putting her first; I was thinking of myself.

Have you been part of a team in which another player was trying to get the attention of a scout? Even if that player is typically considerate of his teammates' strengths, he will likely do everything he can to make that game about himself—to show off his abilities, to get noticed even if it means leaving his teammates out. Transitions are hard, but when we go at them solo and neglect our spouse, we are guilty of the same type of selfishness.

The truth is that often we react selfishly because we feel neglected in those seasons. When I was making sarcastic comments to Irene about her prioritizing the kids, I was feeling neglected. I was afraid in that season that I would always play second fiddle to the kids. I wanted her attention. As selfish as my comments were, they came from a place of fear.

The fear we have of not getting what we want is something that is truly ingrained in us. It's something that society preaches—you better "get yours." But this is toxic to a marriage because it is not based in love.

In part 1 we talked about love being fearless. Let's look again at how the apostle John characterized love: "*Love has no fear*, because perfect love expels all fear. *If we are afraid, it is for fear of punishment*, and this shows that we have not fully experienced his perfect love" (1 John

4:18 NLT, emphasis added). For many of us the "fear of punishment" is simply not getting what we want. Like a child who doesn't want their toy taken away, we switch to more manipulative tactics. We say, "I love you," but our actions expose our fear. My passive-aggressive comments to Irene weren't coming from a place of love; they were coming from a place of fear. Fear of not getting what I wanted.

Friends, I want you to pause here.

Think about the last thing you said to your spouse.

Was it coming from a place of love . . . or fear of not getting what you wanted?

Have you ever played rock, paper, scissors? Rock crushes scissors, scissors cuts paper, and paper covers rock. There's one weapon for each, but not one that can defeat all. Whatever comes against you and your spouse, whatever weapon you're facing, love defeats all.

There is no fear in love, because love has no reason to be afraid.

When you love your spouse with that kind of love, no phase of life is scary. It may be new, it may evoke old emotions you have to navigate together, but none of these things will ever be stronger than love. There is no phase you can't go through when you love your spouse the way Scripture commands us to. In fact, the hard times you walk through together will only make you stronger when you love like this.

FACE YOUR FEARS

We as human beings have a universal fear of change, but where does that fear come from? These transitions in life change us, but why do we so readily assume the worst? In our experience this has most often been a result of our differences. Differences in communication style, differences in needs, differences in our upbringings—they can cause tension whenever it seems the rules have changed or another element has been introduced, and now there's some insecurity.

Often our fears are rational; they come from something we experienced in our past that we don't want to experience again.

Maybe your parenting styles differ and you're afraid of causing your children the same trauma you experienced in your childhood. Instead of working together to find balance, you make your spouse the villain and fight each other.

Maybe a change in job was the beginning of the end of your parents' marriage, and now you don't want your spouse getting that promotion. Your spouse doesn't understand the source of your fear, so it just seems like you don't support their dreams.

Whatever the fear is, love requires us to face it. Only then can we build on our marriage and grow together.

There is a tendency to assume we know best. There's a sense of security in a "known way" of doing things. No matter how much we love one another, it's often altogether too tempting to hold on to our way—to being the one who is "right." The irony is that we have often overanalyzed the other's methods but never even considered why ours are so important to us.

> **Whatever the fear is, love requires us to face it. Only then can we build on our marriage and grow together.**

There was a certain group of people in Scripture who held on to their way of doing things without consideration for a new way. Jesus talked directly to them on a number of occasions—they were known as the Pharisees.

Jesus told them, "Speaking of blindness: Why do you focus on the speck in your brother's eye? Why don't you see the log in your own?" (Luke 6:41 THE VOICE).

We put our spouse under a magnifying glass, but we're afraid to look in the mirror. We need to confront our fear and contain it. Before we determine that our spouse's way of doing things is wrong, we need to evaluate our way: *Where does this fear come from? Why is it so important to me to do this my way?* Often you will be able to trace your fear to a specific origin. Don't keep this information to yourself—make your spouse aware of your feelings. We'll talk more on this later, but this is all part of owning your emotions—it's something we call "extreme ownership."

Some may say they don't want to change or they look at changing as a person as a negative thing, but change is required for positive things such as learning and growing. By definition, we can't improve if we stay the same.

Remember: Love has no fear. And Scripture tells us that love "rejoices with the truth" (1 Corinthians 13:6). Love also does not judge, and it is not arrogant. Which means that when our spouse expresses their opinion or way of doing things, we don't assume a position of superiority. Love should compel us to consider their approach and their feelings. What naturally results is a melding or unification of methods. The two become one, stronger through each new transition.

REAL TALK

Irene

It was Christmas Eve when I boarded that plane, phone in hand, for the first time in forty days. It was one thing to talk about sobriety and recovery at rehab, to bare my soul and trust that my story would be safely received in a room full of recovering addicts whom

I'd watched walk the same journey I was on, but now I was reentering society, and I knew there was a world full of people who would not understand. There were temptations and opportunities to fail.

The fear and shame were overwhelming.

Questions consumed my thoughts on that flight.

What if I mess up—will Jimmy still love me?

Do my kids still respect me?

Will friends abandon me when they learn the truth?

Names and faces flooded my mind, and potential questions only made my anxiety grow.

This transition was the hardest I had ever experienced. The number of uncertainties seemed insurmountable—*where do I even begin? How do I picture a future on the other side when I never imagined being here in the first place?*

It would have been so easy to give up or hide from everyone. To stuff my emotions. That was my past, what I knew. But growth requires change. To become who I was created to be, I had to change.

I'm not going to lie to you and tell you it was easy. It was incredibly hard.

I'm not going to tell you that I immediately felt hopeful. In fact, my first official text message betrayed the shame I felt and asked that no one share that I had been to rehab.

I'm not going to tell you that joy was immediate, because joy comes on the other side of perseverance.

What I will tell you is that *love plays the long game.*

Perseverance isn't about instant gratification. It's about longevity.

"Love never gives up" (1 Corinthians 13:7 NLT).

Love goes the distance and, in time, reaps a harvest far greater and more meaningful than any temporary fix.

Transitions are hard, but if you and your spouse are willing to persevere, they will make you stronger. When I got back from rehab, many obstacles and challenges awaited me. What I never anticipated was the way in which navigating them with Jimmy would actually grow our relationship.

It is important to note that in these seasons of transition, you will need additional grace. Remember the safe place I talked about before? We'll elaborate more on this later, but protecting your bubble is essential for navigating challenging seasons with grace.

When we guarded our bubble, it created a safe place for me to express my fears or weaknesses, and Jimmy was able to meet me there. Love doesn't shout over the noise or force itself into your space: Love whispers and invites. Tune out the distractions of life, turn off your phones and close your computers, and take this opportunity to navigate a transition with your spouse.

TWO-EQUALS-ONE CHALLENGE

What is the latest transition you experienced in your marriage? Are you newlyweds, transitioning from singlehood to married life? If you're new parents, you're making the transition into becoming a mother or father. Maybe it's a new job or the loss of a parent. Whatever it is, write it down.

Independently, write a list of five emotions that you have experienced as a result of this transition.

One of those emotions will likely be fear. No matter how trivial the fear may seem, write it down. Now, using the following diagram, connect memories to each emotion. When you're done, it will look something like the example provided:

Now discuss your diagram with your spouse. Talk about each associated memory. Don't rush this. Discuss ways that you can relate with each other's feelings and ways you can help encourage each other moving forward.

Change is inevitable, but we don't have to go through it alone.

Change is inevitable, but we don't have to go through it alone. Fear often masquerades as a reasonable outcome, a scenario we've convinced ourselves will play out due to a particular change. That's a lie. And when we come together and face these fears, we rebuke the lie.

Fight the feeling that fears are final.

Remember that your spouse is your safe place. The Enemy wants you to believe that your hurt is forever, but change can be healing when we walk out real love in times that would otherwise simply be hard.

PRAYER

Father, thank you for my spouse. Every new transition in life you have already set up for our best. We look to you for guidance, and we come together as one to face our fears. We offer each other honesty and apologize for times when we let fear, rather than love, control us. In Jesus' name, amen.

CHAPTER THIRTEEN

EXTREME OWNERSHIP

Moving ahead requires mapping backward.

W hen was the last time you had a picture of your future together? When
was the last time you imagined what life could be with your spouse?

Often the reason that couples stop dreaming together is because
they've stopped communicating. They've stalled out relationally;
dreaming is something they did when they were newlyweds, but the
mundane has crept in and the hectic pace of life, or the fast track of a
career, has put their marriage on hold.

When we ask couples we are coaching what dreams they have for
their marriage, their answer is usually something vague, such as "I just
want us to be happy," or something material, such as "I hope we're able
to afford a nicer house." These statements are not necessarily bad in
themselves, but they offer no clear vision. *What does "happiness" entail?
Will the nicer house enrich your marriage?*

Without vision, your marriage can't grow. It literally has nowhere
to grow because there is no direction.

REAL TALK

Irene

"What does your marriage look like in five years?"

We were sitting in the counselor's office, and at this point I was taking our marriage one day at a time; I had no thought as to what it might look like in five years. I awkwardly glanced at the carpet, fidgeted with my manicure. I was stalling, and the silence was so deep I could hear the clock as it ticked on the wall.

Then suddenly I had a flashback to our early years. We used to go look at houses together and imagine our future, what it would look like. We would walk hand in hand and fantasize about the journey ahead of us . . . I couldn't remember the last time we had done that.

Have you ever been put on hold with customer service? Once I was left on hold so long that I gave up. I had called to request a refund and ended up losing my money because it wasn't worth the time. I'm afraid this happens in some marriages. The marriage sits on hold for so long that it doesn't feel worth holding on to anymore.

I'll let you in on another truth about those couples I mentioned earlier who want "to be happy" or want "a nicer house." Their statements are often more telling of their triggers or traumas than anything else. The vagueness of their instinctive responses avoids anything personal or specific. What they're often saying is "We haven't really talked about it." This is usually because there's been a breach of trust. Things have been said or done that have derailed the lines of communication; in short, they've been triggered, and it's caused them to distance themselves from one another.

Triggers are like warning signs. We've all been at a restaurant or store and have seen a Caution: Wet Floor sign, put up where the floor was wet from mopping after something was broken or spilled. The sign prevents people from being injured by slipping or falling at that spot. Triggers serve a similar function in marriage. They aren't the trauma itself, but they indicate where there was trauma.

All of us have triggers. Things people have said to us or about us, things people have done that marked us in some way. When a spouse inadvertently sets off a trigger, it's our responsibility to make it known to them.

Throughout our married life, we have moved many times. For Jimmy, as the adventurous, futuristic, let's-do-something-new type of person, this was exciting. But for me this was a trigger. In my childhood, moving was a major source of trauma. Perpetually the "new girl," I longed to be known, to fit in . . . to belong. Instead of embracing who I was, I desperately tried to conform to whatever it seemed would please the current community.

My family's transient lifestyle took an additional toll in the form of my dad's constant traveling. In my earliest years, I remember interpreting my dad's travels as abandonment. As an adult I have come to recognize that he traveled for work—he left to provide for his family. Nonetheless, I felt as though he were leaving me. That I wasn't enough. If I were enough, he would stay with us. Each subsequent move left its mark on me, destabilizing me and heightening my insecurities.

Every time Jimmy and I moved, these feelings rushed back. I would suddenly feel helpless—like I had as a child. As though Jimmy were my parent, telling me to get on board. *Why would you not be supportive of a new adventure? Don't you care that this will be better for our family?*

It took me many years to unpack my feelings—I didn't recognize the source of them until much later. But when I did, I had a responsibility to take ownership of those feelings. "Extreme ownership" is part of adulting. And it might sound like just another boring task, but know this: *ownership is empowering.*

If not held in check, your emotions will run the show. When you take ownership, you will become empowered. Remember how we talked before about emotional health? This is where that comes into play in your relationship with your spouse.

Jimmy

I was once chased by a dog. I was in an area I shouldn't have been, but I swear this animal came out of nowhere. The mangy-looking beast was all teeth as it snarled in my direction. All my survival instincts kicked in, and I ran faster than I ever knew I could, eventually jumping clean over a six-foot fence to get away. I can still hear that nasty bark. Although I got away, a dog barking can still trigger the memory!

You might get away from the dog, but you can't outrun your past. There's no fence that can keep it at bay. The thing about your past is that it has the capacity to enrich your future. It can become your testimony; it can deepen your intimacy, and instead of being a stronghold pulling you backward, it can strengthen your relationship and propel you forward.

But you have to face it.

Stop and think about that.

Are you willing to confront your past so that you and your spouse can have the future God wants for you? To have the future he designed for you?

I highly recommend running from a rabid dog, but running from your past is futile. It'll waste your time, energy, and emotion—and eventually you'll end up stuck there if you don't choose to face it.

For Irene and me, intimacy did not come easily. For the first fifteen years of marriage, however, we didn't even know what the obstacles were that we were up against. Sure, there were symptoms that emerged—addictions, arguments, and general unhappiness. But those were external indicators—what we were really dealing with was much deeper than that.

One day we were in counseling (if you haven't noticed, a lot of breakthroughs were a result of counseling, so I highly recommend it!) and we were talking about my sexual expectations. Very plainly, our counselor asked where a particular expectation came from. I honestly hadn't thought about that. I fumbled a bit. "Well, I guess . . ." Immediately I was hit with the memory.

Ten-year-old me.

Down the street at Brian's house.

That *Penthouse* magazine.

Page 47.

Tears fell down my face. I was overwhelmed by how badly I wanted to unsee that. How badly I wanted to take it back—to have never even been there in the first place.

It was then our counselor said to me, "Take the hand of ten-year-old Jimmy and walk him back."

Sometimes forward progress requires going backward. You can't outrun your past; you have to face it. But when you're able to do this as an adult, you have the ability to walk yourself back to the present—you gain back your freedom.

This is called *mapping*. When our feelings lock us up in the present, we must go backward to get freedom. Think of it like driving without GPS. As much as you may hate Siri's voice, you probably wouldn't attempt to drive in a new area without navigation. I read an article recently about a couple who were driving in the rural West when they lost navigation. Instead of calling a relative or friend to get directions back to civilization, they panicked and dialed 911. Often our triggers make us respond the same way—instead of

You can't outrun your past; you have to face it.

rationally thinking and talking through our emotions, we hit emergency levels of anger or fear.

What we need to do is map that emotion. Ask yourself, *Why did I respond like that?* or *Why did I take that so personally?* Then trace that reaction back in your mind. You might be surprised to find where it lands you. For example:

- Your spouse's tone that immediately gets a rise out of you might trigger a memory of a teacher who made you feel stupid.
- Your spouse's habit that grates on your nerves might remind you of a loved one whom you haven't fully allowed yourself to grieve.
- Your inability to finish things might be a fear of failure that you can trace back to a specific disappointment.

Sometimes, you need to take your younger self by the hand and walk back to your wound.

When you map these emotions, you are able to disengage yourself from the lies. You're able to say, "I am not stupid, and my spouse doesn't think I am either." You're able to grieve that person with your spouse by your side. You're able to reclaim your confidence knowing that one setback doesn't mean you can't succeed.

We've all experienced traumas—they're unavoidable. Statistics show that one in seven children have "experienced child abuse and neglect in the last year."[1] In divorced homes 90 percent of mothers receive custody of their children.[2] Since 1980 at least 20 percent of children have grown up in single-parent homes.[3] And that's not even taking into account the alarming number of children who are victims of sexual abuse. Our world is broken, fam.

And as staggering as these numbers are, there are many other kinds of traumatic life events that scar us well before marriage and make subsequent relationships challenging—events such as financial hardships, broken promises, addictions, or the loss of a loved one. The truth is, as difficult as it is to navigate our triggers together, the sense of wholeness on the other side is a healing that we can't attain on our own.

Allowing yourself to share these breakthroughs with your spouse lets your spouse be part of your own personal growth and grows the intimacy of your relationship. Your past is part of your story, but it's not until we untangle ourselves from the lies that we can freely claim our futures. I learned that a healed Jimmy resulted in a healed sex life, and a present Jimmy always has to be willing to visit the past.

A friend of ours shares Irene's experience of a transient childhood; she remembers places she lived for only a matter of months before being uprooted and moving again. Her husband was the opposite—his parents still lived in his childhood home. He had never experienced selling a house or making a home look "show ready." When they were first married, she started noticing habits that drove her crazy. One in particular was that he would set his clothes on a chair instead of putting them in the hamper or putting them away. Thinking it would help, she moved the hamper closer to the chair he frequently used. But the habit continued. She hinted for a while, but she finally confronted him.

He seemed genuinely surprised by her concern and explained, "They're not dirty enough to add to the laundry, but I've worn them out of the house, so I don't want to put them in my drawers with clean clothes." She did not expect such a response, so, without recourse, she began mentioning other things that he didn't put away and told him how hard she was working to keep their place clean. Emotions rose up, and she didn't even know why, but she started to cry. *Her past was showing up in her present.*

It was in that moment they both realized how different each other's homelife had been growing up. Although neither had been the most tactful in expressing his or her frustration, the conversation had opened a door to feelings they didn't know they carried. He learned about the trauma she held on to—one that affected her more than she had realized. And she learned to take responsibility for those feelings. They now laugh about his "dirty/clean pile," and even though she has not adopted his system, the dialogue was healing. It opened the door to many other conversations later in their marriage that helped them navigate stressful seasons of transition.

THE FIVE *C*S OF EXTREME OWNERSHIP

In his letter to the church in Galatia, Paul urged the church members to take a close look at their own responsibilities—he said to examine yourselves and not compare yourselves to others. In Galatians 6:5 he said, "Each person has his or her own burden to bear *and story to write*" (The Voice). We have an individual responsibility that we alone can carry.

Your spouse doesn't complete you; your spouse complements you. But he or she can do that only if you communicate your needs. That part is entirely up to you. Jimmy and I have found that this involves a process that we call the five *C*s of extreme ownership.

1. **Capture**

   The first *C* is to *capture that thought*—the trigger. In 2 Corinthians 10:5, Paul urged us to "take *every* thought captive" (ESV, emphasis added). You might be thinking, *That's a pretty intense standard!* But it's necessary for emotional health and for the health of your marriage. When you feel that surge of emotion, whether it's dread or shame or anger, log it in. Don't let undealt-with trauma crowd your mind—make it answerable.

Don't immediately assume that the emotion was your spouse's "fault" or that he or she "made" you feel a certain way. If what your spouse said or did triggered a disproportionate response, ask yourself why. Make a point of investigating your own thoughts and feelings. We all have triggers, but we don't all have the same ones; therefore, we can't expect our spouse to know ours in the same way we can't assume we know all of theirs.

2. **Compartmentalize**

The second *C* is to *compartmentalize*—organize your thoughts and feelings. The more you do this, the more clearly you will be able to communicate your needs. It's like cleaning your bedroom. When you were a child, you probably had a parent or guardian who set up where things belonged in your room or how it was supposed to be arranged. This provided an existing structure or format for what your room was supposed to look like.

The trouble with our thought life is that we don't have anyone reminding us where things belong or that they need to be organized. Furthermore, we've often had false narratives told to us along the way that had us putting metaphorical baggage in the wrong drawers. It's important that we sort through our memories and our "stuff" so that we can readily identify the source—where they actually belong. If we don't do this, we will inevitably start misplacing our feelings and projecting them onto our spouse. We will start to associate our feelings of hurt or anger with our spouse rather than with the trigger they may have inadvertently pulled.

Remember: just because one thing is bad or one thing upset you, it doesn't mean everything is bad and your whole marriage is ruined. Don't let a single disagreement ruin your entire day.

3. **Confess**

The third *C* is to *confess*. We need to confess these thoughts—tell your spouse about these emotions and triggers. How else are they going to know?

Have you ever navigated a maze? One of those really tall ones where you can't see over the top in order to find the right path to the heart of the puzzle? You end up wandering into many dead ends before solving it, if you ever do. Sometimes we assume that because we're married, our spouse is going to have the direct path straight to our heart, and that if they make us feel a certain way, it must be on purpose. Meanwhile, our spouse feels as if they've hit a dead end and can't navigate our maze.

Confessing your thoughts and feelings is like sending up a signal to your spouse—it helps redirect the moment and keep your spouse from further triggering you. It gets your relationship back on track. Confession is your work to do—your spouse can't do this part for you. He or she can know your feelings or triggers only if you communicate them, so don't leave your spouse feeling stuck.

4. **Communicate**

The fourth *C* is to *communicate*. Once you've captured, compartmentalized, and confessed your feelings and emotions, it's important to communicate your needs moving forward. How can your spouse help you navigate this trigger?

Remember how I said that Jimmy and I were on opposite pages when it came to moving? I had to tell Jimmy about my feelings and traumas, then communicate my need for dialogue throughout the process. I needed him to be patient when I got frustrated or anxious. I needed him to encourage me but not patronize my feelings. I needed him to validate them and hear out my thoughts and opinions.

Communicate your need; it might be hard, especially if you struggle with codependency, but remember that your spouse is your safe place.

5. **Commit**

The final *C* is to *commit*. Commit to a new normal—imagine your future. As your communication grows, as your intimacy level builds and your emotional health becomes a priority, you will find yourself reimagining your relationship. It will become a source of empowerment.

It's important to be specific in your commitments. Avoid vague statements, such as "I'll be nicer." Instead, focus on specific ways you can support your spouse moving forward.

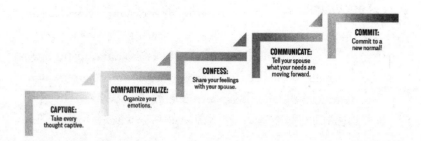

Traumas can be difficult to articulate or even to trace back, but a present trigger is a sign to take a past trip. We've talked about mapping, but it can often be difficult to identify the source of a trigger, especially traumas that are experienced in childhood. This is why even "small things" can be important to address. These experiences are our own—we carry them, which is why we need to take responsibility for them ourselves. Mapping can lead to many breakthroughs. Not only does it allow us to communicate better with our spouse, but it often helps us process through pain.

Our experiences shape our identity—they're part of our unique makeup. In a two-equals-one marriage, your spouse is the one who helps you embrace that identity!

TWO-EQUALS-ONE CHALLENGE

Map that emotion. This may make you uncomfortable, but working independently, ask yourself (do not say anything out loud yet), *When was the last time we were in an argument?* Or, if you've been avoiding an argument for some time, *When was the last time my spouse annoyed me?*

Our experiences shape our identity—they're part of our unique makeup.

Before either of you says anything out loud, take some time to trace that emotion backward. Moving ahead requires mapping backward. Remember, this isn't about what you were arguing about or determining any blame. This is about tracing the origin of your emotion and understanding your trigger. We are not trying to prove anything in this exercise—we're looking to understand.

Ask yourself: *Why did I feel that way?* Was it anger, shame, fear, or grief?

Use the five *C*s and go backward as far as you can. You will know when you've arrived at the source because there will be mental clarity instead of simply emotion.

- **Capture:** Don't let it escape—grab hold of it. Name the emotion.
- **Compartmentalize:** Trace the origin. Just because one thing is bad doesn't mean everything is bad. Separate your trigger from your spouse.
- **Confess:** Tell your spouse how you felt and where the emotion started.
- **Communicate:** Tell your spouse what you need moving forward.
- **Commit:** Commit to a new normal and list specific things you pledge to do for each other.

At this point you and your spouse can take turns sharing your maps. If it helps, have a baton or some object you can pass back and forth to visually represent whose turn it is to talk. Resist the urge to interrupt one another—it's very important you let each other finish. You both want and need to be heard.

As you do this, be as honest and vulnerable as possible. Again, this isn't about being right; it's about being understood. It is important for the health of your relationship that you are both able to share the process. When did you feel triggered? What was the emotion? Ask yourself, *What's coming up for me?* Then walk your spouse back to the origin and express what you need moving forward.

Take ownership.

Avoid accusatory language and focus on your responsibility in the situation.

Then make your commitments to one another.

Be specific and realistic.

If it was a phrase or word that triggered your spouse, it's realistic to say that you won't use that language in your home moving forward. It's not realistic to ask your spouse to never speak to your mother-in-law again! Make sure that what you commit to is attainable and helpful because follow-through builds trust, whereas lack of fulfillment is destructive.

PRAYER

Father, thank you for my spouse. I believe that you created my spouse uniquely and wonderfully, and I want to understand my spouse as you do. Give us both the insight and wisdom to help each other become all that you've created us to be. In Jesus' name, amen.

CHAPTER FOURTEEN

#SAMETEAM

When you learn how to work together,
you learn how to win together.

It's easy to point out the flaws and failures in other people, but it's especially easy to do so in the one person you see *every day*. You watch their habits, notice their quirks—you see the messy, unpolished version. Most of these aren't glaring issues; in fact, most aren't even worth mentioning, but if we ignore our feelings, we invite resentment. The emotions evoked tell us something important about ourselves. This is where having a dialogue to discuss our emotions becomes so important.

Do you ever find yourself expressing frustration to your spouse, starting with the two words "you always"? Those discussions don't typically end productively, do they? We're human, and we've all been there. But we can change, and it starts with changing the script.

REAL TALK

Irene

Dr. Edith Eger is a noted psychiatrist and Holocaust survivor. Her story rises out of a place of incomprehensible evil, a place we know as Auschwitz. Auschwitz wasn't a work camp or ghetto; as horrific as those places were, Auschwitz was worse. It was a Nazi death camp that existed for the sole purpose of exterminating the Jewish race. Eger was rescued when the camp was liberated in 1945. She was found in a pile of dead bodies, her arm wrapped in a Star of David, branded like livestock.

Her story is a firsthand account of what is arguably the greatest evil recorded in modern history. Her family was torn apart, her parents murdered; she even wrote about personal encounters with the sadistic Dr. Mengele himself, also known as "the angel of death." If ever there was a person more acquainted with trauma than Eger, I could not name one. I read her story mostly through tears.

But after a gripping personal narrative, she said something that made me stop. She wrote, "Our painful experiences aren't a liability— they're a gift. They give us perspective and meaning, an opportunity to find our unique purpose and our strength."[1]

I would never recommend playing comparison games, but in that moment, reading her words, I did. I thought about my own victimization and contrasted it to hers. Her experiences, her losses, were exponentially more traumatic because they were all endured on the stage of genocide. Everything she felt, everything she witnessed, every complicated emotion was lived out under the looming shadow of the chimneys of Auschwitz.

How could she say that "our painful experiences are a gift"?

Remember how we talked about extreme ownership? Eger survived the death camp, but what she discovered after survival was how to thrive. The trauma she experienced could have easily led her to a life of solitude with limited relationships—nothing can be lost if it isn't risked, right? No trust can be violated if it isn't given.

Instead, she stated that through "recognizing and taking responsibility for our feelings, we can learn to recognize and take responsibility for our role in the dynamic that shapes our relationships."[2] She talked about how our feelings give us purpose and meaning.

It's not wasted; there is purpose in the pain.

This isn't about excusing the horrors she experienced or giving the perpetrators any kind of pass for their actions; this is about not letting her trauma prevent her from living now. She escaped the Nazis, but without taking ownership of her feelings, she would have remained a prisoner in her own mind. We each have an individual responsibility for what we bring into our marriage.

Jimmy and I have found that having conversation starters can be extremely helpful when navigating triggers. Remember when we talked about communication styles? I'm a verbal processor, so I made a vulnerable request with Jimmy to let me talk through my thoughts with him. It required him to be patient and not bottom-line what I was saying. After establishing that this is how I communicate, there wasn't necessarily a need for me to make a formal request; however, I will still often start conversations with him by saying, "I'm sorry, I'm mapping this."

Our feelings give us purpose and meaning.

This immediately tells him that I haven't fully processed my thoughts. It lets him into my unfiltered, vulnerable space. Because he respects the fact that God created me differently, he waits. He listens. Then he mirrors back to me what he hears that I am saying, allowing me to correct any miscommunications.

Sometimes we need to backtrack. We've all said things in the heat of an argument that we wish we could take back. Words are powerful, and they can leave lasting scars. Many times those scars resurface later, and we have to unlearn them all over again. Jimmy and I have found it important to be *quick to apologize* and *quick to forgive*.

If I catch myself saying "you always," I immediately backtrack. I quickly apologize and say, "I'm sorry I just said that. It wasn't fair."

Jimmy mentioned earlier that he often changes his posture if he knows I need to talk about something serious. At times he even changes his stance and literally gets on the floor if the conversation escalates. This way he doesn't interrupt me, but he indicates to me that what I said may have been hurtful or unfair. It gives me an opportunity to evaluate my words and, if needed, apologize.

Remember what Jimmy said earlier, that it's not about being right, it's about being understood? When we remind ourselves of this truth, it disarms our emotions. We take charge of the situation. We own that emotion, and that emotion is a gift. As Eger said, those painful experiences provide us with meaning and opportunity. Your spouse is the one you see every day—the one who witnesses the mundane and unglamorous. Vulnerability is a tremendous gift when it comes to establishing trust.

When you let your spouse into the broken places and work together to navigate traumas and triggers, you develop what Jimmy and I have already referred to as a safe place. We'll continue to talk on this, but intimacy doesn't start in the bedroom. It starts with trust. It starts with being seen and fully known. The more you learn and understand your spouse, the better you're able to navigate the blueprint for your own growth.

Jimmy

Have you ever played a team sport? I remember the first real jersey I ever had. I was so puffed up seeing my name on the back. I couldn't wait to hear the announcer at the game say it loudly over the speaker every time I made a big play. The recognition, the affirmation, can be like a drug.

There are only a couple of colleges that don't print the individual names on the backs of their football jerseys. Notre Dame and USC are perhaps the most notable examples. Their philosophy is that when you wear a Fighting Irish or a Trojan jersey, that's who you represent. It's not about the individual; it's about the team. I may not watch much college sports, but I can get down with that ideology. In fact, that's how we have to look at getting healthy in marriage. It's not about mine versus yours—it's about us as one. When we look at two equals one this way, we're able to appreciate each other's strengths and not feel jealous when the other's strengths are in the spotlight. Their strengths are in wearing the team jersey—an individual victory is a victory for the team.

Becoming one is not about enduring. If just being married a long time is the goal, it's not worth it. Becoming one is not about surviving. It's about thriving. We each bring deficits into marriage—things we either weren't taught growing up or were miseducated about. It can be uncomfortable as we examine these areas; oftentimes we're oblivious to them.

When we first started marriage counseling, I had every intention of getting my money's worth. I had no problem speaking my mind. This often made Irene upset. Her example growing up was the oppo-site of this. Matter of fact, even though she's the one who has lived all over the world, expressing personal feelings was still foreign to her. One day she spoke up in counseling about how I talked in our sessions. She was frustrated by how openly I communicated my feelings.

Our therapist told her that's what honesty looks like.

Now, I'm not saying this to put my strengths on a pedestal—I can think of a dozen ways she is strong where I am not—but this was an area where her deficit was my strength. What she hadn't learned in childhood, I had on lock. Before we were able to recognize each other's strengths, our differences caused dysfunction. They even made us feel threatened at times and made us resent one another.

But when you learn how to work together, you learn how to win together.

The apostle Paul knew a lot about winning together. He also had a lot to say about humility. If you're not familiar with him, Paul had a long list of credentials. He was no slouch. Yet he called himself a slave and routinely reminded the churches of their indebtedness to God and to one another (Romans 1:1; 6:16; 1 Corinthians 7:23).

In his letter to the church in Rome, Paul had some important things to say about how we ought to love. He said, "Love others *well, and* don't hide behind a mask; love authentically. . . . Be first to honor others *by putting them first*" (Romans 12:9–10 THE VOICE).

When you learn how to work together, you learn how to win together.

This is hardly the message we get from popular culture. Think about the last song you heard or the last commercial you watched; did it encourage you to put your significant other's wants and needs before your own? Did it ask you to lay aside your pride for the sake of another? I doubt it. Advertising campaigns pitch their products by suggesting that "you deserve it." The majority of the Top 20 songs do not talk about helping one another walk through difficult times or accepting limitations.

If you want longevity in your marriage, you must be willing to let down your guard. Like Paul said, "Don't hide behind a mask." But you're also going to have to honor your spouse even when what's behind the mask might feel disappointing. To have harmony in your home, you need both transparency and tribute. Tribute is when appreciation is shown for something valuable.

- When was the last time you expressed your appreciation for your spouse?
- When was the last time you told your spouse something specific that you value about him or her?

THE MARRIAGE CONTINUUM

If we want a thriving marriage, a two-equals-one type of relationship, we have to get to a place where it's natural to honor each other. We call this the marriage continuum, and it is key to understanding if you want lasting harmony.

These are the phases our marriage went through to get from hurting to honoring:

HURTING   HUNTING   HOPING   HELPING   HONORING

Hurting

At some point, most marriages will arrive at a hurting place. When your marriage is hurting, you are well aware that it isn't what you wanted—this isn't what you envisioned marriage to be when you said "I do." At this phase you don't necessarily have solutions, but you aren't happy. This typically leads to hunting.

Hunting

If you're hunting, you're questioning your marriage. You may be wondering if this is how it's supposed to be or even looking for a way out. Hunting also involves seeking help, maybe expressing a willingness to do the work. If you and your spouse are leaning into the work aspect of hunting, you're on your way to hoping.

Hoping

Hoping is where you start getting traction. Where you start feeling joy creep back into your relationship. You see the person you married with fresh eyes again. It may not feel easy yet, but glimpses of what's possible come along and reinvigorate your relationship. This leads to the phase of the marriage continuum where you are able to equip others, including your spouse.

Helping

Up until this point your work will have primarily involved getting yourself healthy. The helping phase of the continuum is where you are able to assist your spouse and even others who are behind you in the marriage continuum. As you are able to do so, you will find it that much more natural to honor one another. We have discovered that helping others helps us too.

Honoring

Honoring your spouse and your marital vows is the goal. There will be seasons of setbacks and struggles—that's part of life—but when we choose to honor our spouse and the promises we made to one another, our marriage exemplifies the love Christ displayed. It's sacrificial and selfless. It's also passionate and free.

Honor the pain. Honor the hurt. Then go help someone else through the marriage continuum. This is how the pain becomes a gift! God will use your pain, your trauma, to heal someone else and help others get to a place where they are able to experience honor in their relationships.

TWO-EQUALS-ONE CHALLENGE

Today's challenge is to openly share a time when your spouse helped you move through the marriage continuum.

- Maybe you were stuck in hurting when your spouse found resources for you both to improve your relationship.
- Maybe there was a moment when your spouse displayed a willingness to do the work and it gave you hope.
- Even the simple act of reading this book together is an effort to build your relationship and should not be overlooked.

Whatever the instance, be specific and take the time to express your appreciation. This is an opportunity to move forward in the marriage continuum as you encourage one another on the journey. Celebrate and champion each other's initiatives. Make sure your spouse knows that you see them and their efforts and that they have positively influenced you. Remember: you're on the same team!

PRAYER

Father, thank you for my spouse. I don't always express how much I value my spouse, and I want to do better. They are uniquely created by you, and I recognize their strengths. I want to win together the way you designed us. I commit to honoring my spouse above myself. In Jesus' name, amen.

CHAPTER FIFTEEN

A BLUEPRINT FOR GROWTH

Your spouse is your blueprint for growth.

Knowledge is power. The reverse is also true, however. Ignorance is a prison. There are things we have intuited or experienced in our past that we aren't consciously aware of, but they're affecting our behavior in negative ways.

When you aren't acquainted with something, you have no basis to form ideas about it. That's why the first several years of a person's life are called "formative years"—they are when you're forming ideas and gaining building blocks to understanding the world around you.

For some of you, your introduction has unknowingly become your instruction. What you learned or experienced, especially in those early foundational years, altered your perceived reality.

And that introduction became a way, a wound, or a weapon:

- Maybe it was an overbearing parent—you grew up thinking that was normal behavior, and now you're arguing with your spouse because your spouse parents differently.

191

- Maybe a boyfriend cheated on you, and now you are distrustful when your husband is around other women.
- Maybe your childhood taught you that to survive you had to manipulate the people around you, and now that toxic behavior has created a major rift between you and your spouse.

Whatever you saw then, whatever you experienced or felt, is showing up today. Your introduction has become your instruction.

REAL TALK

Jimmy

Have you ever tried to build one of those complicated LEGO kits? There's a reason they give you a manual-sized instruction book (book, not book*let*). You can have all the tiny colored pieces, all the design stickers, but it will not turn out the way it's supposed to if the instructions are incomplete or incorrect. You may get relatively close, but more than likely all you'll have in the end is a mess to clean up.

Your spouse is your blueprint for growth. Your spouse is there to help you figure out where the pieces go—or if they belong at all. It's not about judgment or who had the better upbringing or who has more baggage. It's about helping each other become who God created each of you to be so that, together, you make a stronger unit.

Irene and I recently built a house. As all homes do, it required a blueprint. Every contractor, construction worker, and plumber referenced this blueprint; deviating from the plan would result in false instructions. Mistakes are made when we don't respect the design.

Likewise, you need to respect your spouse's design and help one another identify where false instruction has resulted in hurt or trauma.

You and your spouse are a team, and it is essential to operate as one. In order to do so, you must evaluate any toxic introductions in your life. Identifying the false instructions that you've been following is about finding freedom, not fault. It's time to face your fears because love is stronger than fear—love is the only safe place to navigate your past so that you can be free in your future.

Irene

Have you ever taken a personality test? I am such a geek about that stuff—I could study them all day long and not get bored. There's so much they tell us about how our minds work and how we process experiences and information. One thing I've learned is that there's a difference between intrinsic behavior and learned behavior. Something can be part of your behavior that isn't truly part of your identity.

A common thread among any of the tests I've taken (and I have taken many) is that I am a peacemaker. Being a peacemaker is *intrinsically* part of my identity. No matter where—home or work—I assume the task of creating harmony and unity. It's something God placed in me that has always been a part of who I am. It's a gift that I'm uniquely able to bring into our marriage, and it makes us stronger. And let me tell you, the feeling of being able to help your spouse from a place of your intrinsic strength is incredible! To link up as a unit and empower one another is a rush.

Stuffing my emotions is *learned* behavior—it's not healthy, but it was ingrained in me as a child. My introduction to dealing with emotions became my instruction. It's something I learned, something I was taught, whether consciously or subconsciously. And it's something I am responsible to unlearn. We all have intrinsic and learned behaviors. They're aspects of our identities that we are better able to navigate as we develop our emotional intelligence.

Some learned behaviors are simply tools that help us compensate in areas of weakness; others are harmful habits or patterns that we either were taught or intuited along the way in our development. We are responsible as adults to unlearn the latter.

Since you've been married, I'm sure you've been told that "you've changed." I want to be clear here—*that's not necessarily a bad thing!* In fact, growth requires change. The important part is knowing yourself well enough to make sure that the areas in which you change are the negative learned behaviors. Jimmy has helped me enormously in learning how to express my needs and feelings. That's something he was uniquely equipped to do. Scripture tells us, "Each of you should use whatever gift you have received to serve others, as faithful stewards of God's grace in its various forms" (1 Peter 4:10).

In his grace, God gave us ways to help each other reach our fullest potential. Jimmy's gift and ability to confidently express his emotions and needs fits perfectly in the space where I struggle—it is strength where I am weak, but only when we work together. As a result of our applying this two-equals-one principle, I've become more vocal and assertive, which in turn leads me to a more emotionally healthy place where I can respond and relate to the needs of others. This is the skill of emotional health in practice—this is growing in love.

God gave us ways to help each other reach our fullest potential.

In 1 Corinthians, Paul talked about what it means to grow as a person, to grow in love. He said, "When I was a child, I spoke and thought and reasoned as a child. But when I grew up, I put away childish things" (13:11 NLT). I know that adulthood comes with a heap of responsibility. If I'm honest, sometimes I find myself feeling a twinge of envy for the freedom I see in little children! But the reality is that along with the depth of responsibility comes greater beauty; our experiences of love and what it really means to love become so much clearer and more meaningful.

There is nothing more worthwhile than love.

Nothing that could bring a greater return.

Nothing that will outlast.

So don't be afraid of change. Use the tools we've talked about to navigate your feelings. To communicate your feelings. And as you're doing so, identify whether that habit or tendency is something that maybe you inadvertently picked up along the way; perhaps it's not worth carrying anymore.

UNIQUELY EQUIPPED TO HELP YOUR SPOUSE

When you're able to name your intrinsic behaviors, it can clarify ways in which you are uniquely equipped to help your spouse. Maybe you are a great conversationalist, but your spouse is socially awkward. Instead of seeing your spouse as social deadweight and avoiding large gatherings, see it as an opportunity to band together. By owning your spouse's differences, your confidence will spark curiosity and your genius at conversation will provide your spouse with time to collect his or her thoughts, making what your spouse contributes all the more valuable. In short, you'll be more interesting together than you ever were apart!

Maybe you're extremely budgeted and keep a tight rein on finances, but your spouse is generous to a fault. Help each other and embrace the feeling of being challenged. You will find balance where independently there might have been issues.

As we've mentioned before, we all also have learned behaviors. While some of these we are consciously aware of and others require processing, it's nonetheless important to examine them. Even habits as seemingly insignificant as compulsively brushing your teeth can be an indicator of a learned behavior formed as a result of trauma.

Because we care about our spouse, we want them to have a high opinion of us. Part of the reason we resist introspection or get defensive with each other is because we are trying to protect the image our spouse has of us. As you unpack these learned behaviors, be gentle with one another. Use care in how you address them and cushion any negative comment with praise. If you want to bring out the best in your husband or wife, you have to call out the best.

Scripture tells us, "Every good gift and every perfect gift is from above" (James 1:17 ESV). It's important to celebrate each other's strengths and recognize where those strengths came from. Remember that the gifts God gave your spouse are meant to bless you as well! It's easy to envy the gifts we see in our spouse and get caught in a comparison trap—resist this. This is not an us-versus-them situation. It's a two-equals-one situation. Being aware of your spouse's strengths doesn't mean ignoring or downplaying your own. It's part of the plan, the blueprint.

You are each other's blueprint for growth.

TWO-EQUALS-ONE CHALLENGE

Take some time to celebrate the intrinsic gifts you've observed in your spouse. There is a list in the back of this book of personality assessments, and if you haven't done so already, we highly recommend taking them, but for the purpose of this exercise, your observations will suffice.

This is an opportunity to talk about your spouse's qualities and natural talents. To note specific instances when your spouse's gifts have positively affected you.

The more specific, the better. Don't be defensive if your spouse's strength is also your weakness—this is part of the equation. Remember: your spouse's strength is a gift that you married! It's meant to complement you, not compete with you.

Part 1: Your Spouse's Strengths

Either grab a notebook or pull out your phone and start a new note. Write your spouse's name and then the word *strengths*. Spend the next three minutes writing out three of your spouse's strengths.

Now look at your spouse and take turns telling each other about your list. Don't rush this process—it can be tempting to just name each one, but be descriptive. It can be helpful to add the phrase "for example." You might say, "You are great at raising the kids. For example, last week I noticed you . . ." .

This may feel awkward at first, but it's a great exercise to do on a regular basis. Seeing your spouse's strengths and saying them out loud is not something we naturally do day in and day out, but it is essential for navigating differences. Don't be discouraged if it feels strained at first. Think of it like a muscle—like going to the gym, it's challenging at first, but with practice, it gets easier, and you reap a benefit that is actually visible.

Part 2: Your Own Weaknesses

If you thought talking about strengths was awkward, you're probably cringing at the thought of talking about weaknesses! But hang in there with us. This exercise requires some humility and the understanding that, together, your weaknesses are an opportunity to know, love, and appreciate each other more. Don't feel as though you have to be perfect—we all have weaknesses, and a huge part of this marriage equation is embracing each other's weaknesses.

For this part, create a new category, but this time it's for yourself. Instead of pointing out your spouse's weaknesses, make a list of three of your own shortcomings.

Now share your list with your spouse, owning your weaknesses and not trying to explain them or make excuses. This exercise can be a great opportunity to own up to things you might typically avoid admitting. For example, "One of my weaknesses is staying present and really listening when you talk. Last night when you were talking about your day—not trying to make an excuse—I was distracted by work. I know I could've done a better job being in that conversation with you."

After you talk through your strengths and weaknesses, pay attention to how you feel. Chances are you feel closer as a couple than you have in a long time.

Part 3: Observed Behavior

The next part of this challenge may require some time to process. Don't rush it. This is where you each identify a potentially learned behavior you've observed in your spouse. This is not about making an accusation—all you're doing is observing a behavior and telling your spouse how you feel.

Note: What may seem odd to you may actually reflect more about your own upbringing than theirs.

Some friends of ours once did this exercise, and the wife wrote that her husband's encouraging them to fast (the Christian practice of abstaining from specific foods in order to prioritize God) led her to feeling pressured and self-conscious about her weight.

What she couldn't see prior to talking through her feelings was that her previous battles with eating disorders had clouded her perspective on fasting. What he saw as a purely spiritual exercise was for her a diet; while he was resisting some of his favorite foods and thereby clearing his heart and mind, she was resisting the foods but simultaneously counting calories. Diet was a trigger that had in the past sent her into a spiral. After their conversation they were able to navigate fasting together by avoiding fasts that were strictly food-based.

What you write may end up telling you something about yourself that you didn't see before. Approach what you observe with humility and be sure to give your spouse time to process. It's possible that your spouse has never considered his or her behavior "abnormal."

Be sure to own your own emotions.

Fill in the blanks in this sentence:

"When I see you do or say _____, I feel _____."

After you read each other's sentences, take a moment to reflect on the behavior that your spouse has observed. Try to find a way to relate to your spouse's emotion. Avoid becoming defensive—remember that your spouse is for you. Listen and consider what motivates your behavior. Then consider where you may have learned this behavior.

Is it intrinsic or is it something you can unlearn?

These conversations are part of the blueprint—they build into harder conversations that are necessary when navigating transitions. Ever watched a home being constructed? Like we talked about earlier, before the builders can even lay the foundation, there needs to be a blueprint—a map charting the way. These conversations are putting ink on the paper so that you can build toward longevity and create something lasting.

PRAYER

Father, thank you for my spouse. I am so thankful for the way you have uniquely created each of us—we are stronger together because of our individual giftings. Help us to complement each other and celebrate one another's gifts. Help us also to process through behaviors that are not from you. We want to honor you and each other in everything we do. In Jesus' name, amen.

CHAPTER SIXTEEN

JOINT COMPOUND

You will never have the spouse you
want until you love the one you have.

H ave you ever visited the Louvre Museum in Paris? Many people
don't realize that the Louvre is more than an art museum—it
began as a palace in the sixteenth century, and subsequent kings added
on to the structure with their own grand modifications. As a result, the
palace is a mile-long composition of winding hallways and elaborate
wings that lead to more hallways. It's so expansive, in fact, that they
give you a map upon entry. What we didn't realize when we visited is
that the map couldn't possibly fit the actual blueprint or show all the
existing rooms, so as we wandered, we discovered rooms that weren't
on the map.

Many of us have given our spouse a map like this—we were transparent about the main things, those are all well marked. But as you
work through the process of extreme ownership with your spouse, you
will find there are things that aren't on your original map. They're

not something you're intentional about featuring. In fact, there will be some things that you would rather not have to walk your spouse through. But they're still part of who you are, and often they're essential to fully understanding you.

Sometimes we don't understand or recall the original blueprints, and the idea of revisiting an area means opening the door to painful emotions—we block out these parts because if we start down that hallway, we aren't sure of everything that we will find.

Many people visit the Louvre to see the *Mona Lisa* or some other well-known masterpiece. They don't even bother meandering past the highlighted exhibits or traveling attractions. They're typical tourists, staying long enough to get a picture and jot down some notes to tell friends back home, but they don't go any further. Here's the thing: Your marriage is not the Louvre, and your spouse is not meant to be a tourist in your life. Tourists eventually pack their bags and leave. For your marriage to last, you have to let your spouse in—you have to walk down the hallways of your past together.

Your spouse is not meant to be a tourist in your life.

REAL TALK

Irene

I'll never forget Hawaii. It was supposed to be a dream vacation.

We were in counseling, doing the intensives before I committed to rehab. We had gotten the warnings—counselors telling us that "it will get worse before it gets better," but we had seen some progress. We were starting to feel hopeful. Cautiously hopeful, but, nonetheless, there were visions of what our life could look like. I wanted so badly to make Jimmy happy—I wanted him to love me, all of me, but I knew I was still holding back. I was afraid that if I was honest with him, he would leave.

At this point in our marriage, *we had achieved peace for the sake of peace, not for the sake of each other.* We had worked through some of our hang-ups and hurts, but we were avoiding the kind of honesty that leaves you exposed. The kind of honesty that has nothing to hide.

I was putting on a show that vacation. Don't misunderstand, I was genuinely trying; I didn't want to let Jimmy or my family down, but I simply wasn't ready or willing to put down that last barrier—that last mask.

I had a flower in my hair, I was dancing—the picture of happiness. The sun-soaked sands of Hawaii glowed in the setting radiance. Rainbows of light engulfed us until we were lit only by the fire of tiki torches. But the romance of the scene couldn't hide my problem. I had been drinking and Jimmy saw through my charade. I had the intention of quitting alcohol, but the glimmer of what we dreamed of, that glimmer of a real, intimate connection, was overwhelmed by my urge to drink.

Jimmy loved my dancing, he loved my smiles, he loved the picture I made against the brilliant colors of this island . . . but he couldn't live with the lies, and he knew I had been drinking.

Alcohol still had a grip on me. It was still consuming my thoughts and causing me to sneak around, hiding my addiction. That night after the luau it all came crashing down around us. It felt as if we had set fire to all the exits in an attempt to stay married, to keep us from leaving, only to realize that we were the cause of our own destruction. All the half-truths and masks that we had held on to for so long had betrayed us, and that night we got into the most explosive fight of our married life.

Hope had evaporated on the beach that day.

What Jimmy and I have learned (albeit the hard way) is that God wants to turn your traumas and tragedies into trophies. He wants to give you victory. He wants to turn your mess into a masterpiece! But it will require you and your spouse to be equally committed. Are you willing to go the distance?

Jimmy

Love can make you crazy. There have been times in our marriage when I did things or said things that made me look or sound flat-out crazy. These actions were a result of misguided passion. The feelings I had for Irene were real—too real. The idea that there was a limitation or a wall between her and me made me crazy.

If you're a parent, you know that the minute you tell your child (especially if he or she is a toddler) not to do something, it will become the one thing they want to do. If you take a toy away, they will fixate on that toy until it becomes the only toy they want to play with. It's human nature to resist boundaries, going all the way back to Adam and Eve. Now, this childlike behavior is something we have to train out, but I think there's also a side to our humanity that yearns for the freedom of the garden of Eden.

God created mankind free. They were so free, in fact, that they didn't even need clothing! There was no separation, no disguise or limitation; Adam and Eve were completely vulnerable with each other. That was God's design.

Hawaii showcased how many layers were still between Irene and me, and it was killing our intimacy. We both were still so guarded, and what I couldn't see was that before we could have the intimacy I craved, we had to let go. And letting go is more than just being honest.

Letting go also means that you stop trying to fit your spouse into a mold—you stop trying to make them into an idea you have in your head. You have to be willing to accept your spouse for who they are before they can become all God designed them to be—but let me tell you something: the person God has in mind, the identity he formed for them, is infinitely better than the one in your head.

A wise friend once told me to stop complaining about Irene. We were in a truly painful season, and it was hard to hear, but this friend has the relational equity to speak into my life, and that day he said exactly what I needed to hear. He said to me, "You will never have the wife you want until you love the one you have."

This is true for all of us. Until we love the one we're married to right now, we will always be chained to the fantasy or illusion in our mind. Your spouse is a human who comes with scars and baggage. But Scripture tells us that love covers a multitude of sins. Peter said this: "Above all, keep loving one another earnestly, since love covers a multitude of sins" (1 Peter 4:8 ESV). That word *earnestly* is important. It suggests a serious, deliberate sense of purpose. The *Oxford English Dictionary* uses the synonym "gravely impassioned."[1]

Are you gravely impassioned about loving your spouse?

When we love with that kind of purpose, it covers the sins we find so distracting—it removes the baggage from the equation. Do we deal with the sin? Yes. Do we walk and talk through the trauma? Absolutely. But without that intentional kind of love, none of it makes a difference.

LOVE COMES FIRST... AND LAST

Remember how we said love comes first? Truthfully, it also comes last. Love is the beginning and the end. I thought loving Irene through her recovery was for her, but it came full circle. It wasn't until after her recovery—watching her strength and her determination—that I had the courage to deal with my addiction to food. Her intentional love played out in front of our family and brought healing. Healing I didn't know I needed. If she hadn't been by my side in the hospital, walking with me through my weight-loss surgery and physical therapy, I doubt I would be here. Love knew the blueprint, even when we didn't. When we stopped trying to diagnose ourselves and each other and just loved one another intentionally, the pieces came together.

We're not suggesting any part of it is easy, but healing and wholeness happen only when we show our spouse "gravely impassioned," earnest love. Paul told us that love "does not insist on its own way" (1 Corinthians 13:5 ESV). Stop acting like you know everything. It can be easy to think that because we see what's going on from the outside, we can make a more informed decision. We would be, at best, treating symptoms or prescribing painkillers.

You can't predict the future.

You don't know your spouse better than their Creator does.

Let go.

Don't insist on your life or your marriage or your spouse conforming to your way. Let go. When you do, you will find freedom. You will find that the person God created is far bigger and more incredible than the one you invented.

THE JOURNEY OF HEALING

The healing process is a journey. For us there were good and bad mile markers. Have you ever been on a long road trip? Usually there are markers and places along the way that become like monuments and remind you of a significant place or event. Something you take a funny picture of and tell friends and family about. Maybe it's a favorite local dive restaurant that serves the best comfort food, or a bridge that makes you nauseated because it's so high, or an unexpected sight that makes for a fun anecdote later.

Life has markers like this, but sometimes they mark events that are painful. For us that looked like holes punched in the wall in anger. That looked like every hiding spot for alcohol. That looked like a couch that had been the spot of many of our worst arguments.

The healing process is a journey.

Part of the healing process is to reclaim the territory the Enemy has stolen. In Psalm 110, David quoted God and spoke a promise over himself. God told David, "I [will] make your enemies a footstool for your feet" (v. 1). Friends, we don't battle flesh and blood (Ephesians 6:12). We often take out our frustrations on other people, on our spouses in particular, but they are not the enemy. The Enemy comes at us in our areas of weakness, the places we're most likely to make a mistake and feel shame. He attacks us in the places we want to hide from other people.

What we want you to know is that your struggles and your weaknesses can become your platform and part of becoming who you were created to be—they can become the footstool David was talking about. The same areas where you were knocked down before can become the places where God builds you up.

MORE REAL TALK

Irene

As we started to get healthy, we recognized the need to reclaim our home and more—we're talking about intentional action here. So

Jimmy and I rolled up our sleeves and went to work. We went around the house and prayed over the drywall we patched. Jimmy confronted the anger that caused the damage, and we rebuked the lies even as we slathered the walls in joint compound, working the spackle into every gouged-out crevice.

We spoke Scripture over the wounds:

- Words of redemption: "With your unfailing love you lead the people you have redeemed" (Exodus 15:13 NLT).
- Words of affirmation: "I've redeemed you. I've called your name. You're mine. . . . *That's* how much I love you! I'd sell off the whole world to get you back, trade the creation just for you" (Isaiah 43:1, 4 MSG).
- Words of forgiveness: "He has removed our sins as far from us as the east is from the west" (Psalm 103:12 NLT).
- Words of promise: "Finally, I confessed all my sins to you and stopped trying to hide my guilt. I said to myself, 'I will confess my rebellion to the LORD.' And you forgave me! All my guilt is gone" (Psalm 32:5 NLT).

We prayed together in every place that used to conceal secrets. I confessed every place I had previously used to hide alcohol, and we prayed over the pain—no more secrets, no more hiding. Vulnerable before one another.

No more hiding means that we are free.

Confession means we are known.

We anointed our space and reclaimed what had been taken.

We hedged what we valued on a spiritual level, knowing that when we stand together on his promises, there is no power greater.

Jimmy

A few years ago, we had the opportunity to revisit Hawaii. There was a moment of hesitancy at the thought of our previous experience— painful memories surged back. This time, however, we didn't avoid dealing with the pain or the uncomfortable emotions. We had learned that love is a lot like joint compound—it finds the flaws and fills the voids. It wasn't designed for a perfect space but rather for the broken places.

We've learned that the only way forward is through, so instead of avoiding, we took back Hawaii. We went—intentionally—to all of those places where we had said all of those hateful words and spoke truth over the lies. We spoke affirmations over one another. We reclaimed our marriage through loving intentionally.

Love covers a multitude of sins.

Love covers our home.

Love covers each other.

TWO-EQUALS-ONE CHALLENGE

It's time to reclaim some territory.

Make a list together of places, starting in your home, that evoke a painful memory in your relationship. Be honest and vulnerable with each other as you make this list. This is not about settling old scores— this is about coming together and reclaiming your marriage.

- Go around to each place you listed and pray together over them.
- Be specific.

- Denounce any lies or hurtful words thrown in the heat of an argument.
- Replace each with a truth and an affirmation.

Don't rush through this. This is your opportunity to honor one another and show the impassioned love that God commands us to have for each other.

PRAYER

Father, thank you for my spouse. I want to honor you in our marriage in the way that I love my spouse. I choose to be intentional and to demonstrate my love for my spouse in every way I can. I invite your presence as my spouse and I reclaim our home and our marriage. In Jesus' name, amen.

CHAPTER SEVENTEEN

BOUNDARIES

Boundaries aren't bad; they're a blessing!

As you identify the sources of your trauma, as you grow in your emotional health, and as you learn your spouse's triggers, you will inevitably find places where you need boundaries—areas that need guardrails.

Security measures are a natural response to potential threats. The White House and Buckingham Palace have fences and other security barriers in place that create a boundary between the property and the public. This doesn't mean that the gates never open, but there is a boundary in place so that traffic is carefully monitored and the residence is not violated. If someone has posed a threat in the past, they will likely be denied entry. In the same way, the "threats" that you identify, you may need to detach from in love.

REAL TALK

Irene

For me, post-recovery, there were friends and even other pastors I had to detach from. What I found was that not everyone whom I had allowed into my life previously respected the fact that I am an alcoholic. Some of you reading this will argue that I should be speaking in past tense, but I will, for the rest of my life, be working on my sobriety. I am sober, but I will never become complacent about that. What that means is that I need to detach from anyone who is potentially a stumbling block for me.

Some of you have experienced abuse at the hands of someone close to you. Even if reparations have been made and forgiveness has been offered, you will still need to be mindful of your boundaries. To detach doesn't necessarily mean to block completely. Just like the fences we mentioned earlier, some people will be denied entry while others may simply be granted limited access.

Boundaries will look different depending on your traumas and triggers.

This wasn't always an easy space to navigate for Jimmy and me. Some of the people I needed to detach from were working relationships. People who were connected, who could potentially grow our platform and our careers. But Jimmy and I made a choice—to put each other first.

Some of the boundaries we put up are actually to keep us out. Have you ever been to the Grand Canyon? If you have, you've seen the teeny-tiny, wide-open guardrail that lines the perimeter of a cliff so high you can't really even make out the canyon floor. The first time a friend of mine went, she said that her knees felt weak as she glanced over the edge. As wimpy as the guardrail was, it stood there to remind visitors of the danger. On average, two to three people a year fall to their deaths here—there must be respect for the edge.[1] In the same way, areas that cause us to stumble or fall should have

> **Boundaries will look different depending on your traumas and triggers.**

guardrails. I'm not going to hang out in a bar after work—there is a guardrail in place in my life, and I put it there.

Whatever is a limitation or potential stumbling block for you, you need to communicate it with your spouse. Part of being each other's blueprint for growth is helping to alleviate or reduce stress. You do that by showing awareness for their limitations.

Guardrails aren't baby gates. This isn't about limiting your life or treating you like a child. This is about ownership. This is about making deliberate choices in your life that will ensure you have the future you want. For some of you, that might mean cutting up your credit cards or making the racetrack off-limits. For some it may be as simple as deleting an app on your phone or not listening to a particular kind of music.

The Grand Canyon is breathtaking, but you can't enjoy it if you're plummeting to your death. The same is true of the danger areas in our life. Guardrails exist to ensure we can enjoy all that God has given us, with respect to the areas that for us are potentially dangerous.

Jimmy

Proverbs 4:23 tells us, "*Above all else*, watch over your heart; diligently guard it because from a sincere and pure heart come the good and noble things of life" (THE VOICE). In the ancient world, at the time this psalm was written, people made no distinction between the heart and the mind in terms of decision-making.[2] Today it's easy to get scientific and look at the heart as an organ and make its function purely biological. But there's a whole metaphysical side to our created being, and we do answer for the motives of our heart.

Our motives and our feelings drive our behaviors. We have to watch over our hearts if we want to have the future God wants for us. But it's not simply about reacting—it's about being proactive.

In football a good defense is just as important as a good offense. Everyone loves making a touchdown, scoring points, and celebrating. But to win you have to be able to stop the opposing team from scoring, and that requires defensive strategy. One player that typically gets overlooked is the free safety. This position lines up the deepest and has to get a good read on what the other team is about to do. They relay this to their defensive teammates. A good free safety is able to prepare for whatever play the opposition is about to run and shut it down. The legendary 1985 Chicago Bears managed to allow only seven yards of rushing the entire Super Bowl. Their opponent literally could not move against them. This should be our goal when setting up our own defensive strategy.

Our motives and our feelings drive our behaviors.

We need to be able to neutralize any threats coming against our marriage.

So what does that look like? For Irene and me it starts with guarding our time. Our lifestyle requires a lot of travel, and it can be easy to become so busy that we compromise date nights or quality time. The first line of defense we set up is around the two of us. We've found that we need our time to check in on a regular basis and to ensure that we are communicating and meeting one another's needs.

We set up an additional level of protection around our family. This particular line of defense goes through transitions as the kids get older and our role as parents inevitably changes. We're currently experiencing a season of change in terms of boundaries with our adult children. It has required plenty of communication and the resolution that we always prioritize our safe place.

Each subsequent barrier is carefully communicated with each other to ensure that both our needs are being met. In some cases, a boundary was put in place simply because a relationship was draining one or both of us. That's right: if one of us finds a particular relationship exhausting or difficult, whether it's because of a simple personality clash or tension over an entirely different belief system, we put a boundary in place.

If it concerns your spouse, it should concern you too.

In some cases, boundaries are about distancing ourselves from people who don't share our values or priorities. We choose not to carry people who don't champion our goals or support us.

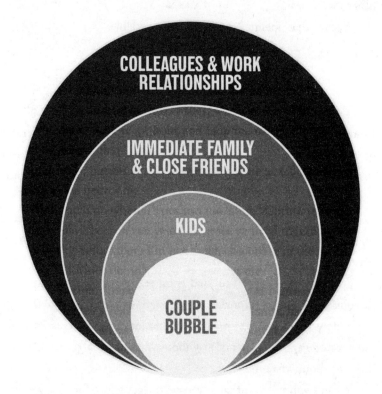

This is not about judging everyone around you. Be careful of judging people who sin differently than you. Not everyone shares the same struggles, but we all struggle. Not everyone is going to understand alcoholism or my struggle with pornography. That's okay—they don't need to. There are plenty of sin behaviors I don't understand either, but I can always respect boundaries. I can always respect a person doing their best to guard their heart.

As you set up your plan to defend your family, it is essential you think as a team. This is where an awareness of your differences—of your strengths and weaknesses—becomes essential. It's also where it becomes important to champion each other's strengths and guard each other's weaknesses.

A team that operates this way is unstoppable.

BEAR ONE ANOTHER'S BURDENS

Boundaries can be hard to accept. Especially if a boundary is a result of your spouse's weakness, not your own. But we have to change our thinking on this. Scripture commands us to "bear one another's burdens" (Galatians 6:2 ESV). Paul was telling the church in Galatia to stop thinking of themselves and to think instead as a unit. He went on to tell them, "If you think you are too good for that, you are badly deceived" (6:3 MSG).

Strong words, right? Paul had good reason to talk this way. Our responsibility is to one another—by design. Let us put it like this: In the same way we weren't created for isolation, we were created to be there for one another. It's not just about what you *get* from a relationship, it's about what you *give*.

Society will tell you that you have to "get yours" or that you can "pull yourselves up by your own bootstraps," but this is a deception of the Enemy. Yes, work on yourself and grow in your own individual maturity. Yes, grow in your emotional intelligence.

But do so to better help others.

The goal is to grow as a unit—as a team. To do so we have to account for each other. If you spend much time in the gym, you know that when you lift weights, you don't start out benching 225 pounds. (In reality, most never get close to this number!) When you start training, you add weight gradually as you build muscle. There are spotters—people who are there to make sure you don't attempt to do more than you're able. Because risk of injury is high, we tend to be more receptive to help. We are willing to stop when we've hit our limit.

These lines often get blurry when it's something we don't want to stop.

This is where boundaries can cause friction. We're usually okay when it's quitting time at the gym, but when it comes to saying no to a certain friend group or activity, it's easy to become resentful. The reality is that we might be more than capable of taking on more weight, but our spouse is about to drop. As a team we need to know when to pause and prioritize the person we married.

Before you get frustrated by limitations, remember this: Boundaries aren't always a permanent fixture. We respect them because we know they exist to protect us, but sometimes it's about a season. It's about working through something together so that a stumbling block becomes nothing more than a memory.

Boundaries are often about navigating transitions. Maybe you're in a season of health challenges or you're not feeling fulfilled physically or sexually in your marriage. It's easy to start to lean on other relationships to vent your frustration instead of talking to your spouse, but set healthy boundaries in place. Remember: Love plays the long game. Seasons change, but the way you handle this transition will set you up to be either stronger on the other side or strained.

It's also important to remember that there will be differing abilities. Some people have tremendous upper-body strength, while others crush leg day. You're stronger together, but only when you operate as one.

Paul said that if we think we're too good to help each other, that we're somehow above everyone else, we're "badly deceived." That's because we were meant to have a counterpart.

When you live selfishly, thinking about yourself first, you will inevitably be lonely. But when you live generously, that's when you will find that your relationships thrive. Love casts out fear; it despises shame. Boundaries aren't bad; they're a blessing! You were meant for more, and your marriage can be more.

TWO-EQUALS-ONE CHALLENGE

Take some time today to talk with your spouse about areas that need boundaries in your life. Individually, write out areas that are a cause of stumbling for you. They don't have to be sin issues; they can simply be things that cause you frustration, things that could potentially invade your safe place. Relationships that you find draining, tasks that you would like to share the responsibility for, or maybe something with regard to your budget. Take turns talking through your lists.

Now make a plan to put boundaries in place. Write down ways you can support one another and ensure that you are both cared for.

PRAYER

Father, thank you for my spouse. I want to make sure that what we do in life embraces our strengths and considers our weaknesses. We desire to honor you in all that we do and to love one another unselfishly. In Jesus' name, amen.

CHAPTER EIGHTEEN

CONTROL + ALT + DELETE

It's time to press the Reset button
and wipe the slate clean.

Are you tired of hearing "I'm sorry" with no change in behavior? Those two powerful words can breathe life back into relationships—that is, until they get disconnected from the action we think should follow them. "I'm sorry" quickly loses its power when we hear it more than see it in our marriages.

The longer you're married, the more times you will have the opportunity to forgive. Throughout the course of your marriage, there will be many phases—and these phases will come with conflict, misunderstanding, and varying levels of intimacy and optimism. Because you're human, things will inevitably be said or done that require forgiveness in order to move forward.

Many couples get stuck in a cycle of resentment and shame when there is unresolved pain.

> **The longer you're married, the more times you will have the opportunity to forgive.**

What do you do when it seems your spouse has made more withdrawals than deposits in a particular area? Or when he or she has emptied the "I forgive you" reserve and the intimacy slowly cycles into contempt? This is an equation for unforgiveness to multiply in your marriage.

REAL TALK

Irene

I have personally experienced this cycle. I found it easier to skew negative and fixate on Jimmy's faults. No matter how much I loved him, I found myself keeping a mental tally of the times I'd had to forgive him.

My attitude became hostile, full of resentment, and I was blinded by the feeling that it was all his fault. I couldn't see my own issue: the issue of built-up resentment. Like a clogged gutter, the problem is debris in the way of rain washing it clean. As long as there's no rain, you can't see it, so it's easy to ignore.

The thing about a clogged gutter is that its function isn't designed for fair weather—gutters are designed for rain. When there is debris blocking the funnel of water through the channel, gutters are pretty pointless. So is saying "I forgive you" if you're holding on to resentment. Resentment will hold you back, hindering your relationship.

But how do you break that cycle? We naturally know how to hold on to our grievances, but how do you let go?

One day I was speaking to my counselor, and she gave me a challenge. She told me to pause three times a day and spend a few minutes listing the things I love about Jimmy. Now, I have to be honest: In the beginning, that challenge was a *challenge*. It wasn't easy! Of course, there are countless things I loved about Jimmy, but those weren't the things my frustration wanted to focus on.

This challenge might seem like a silly idea. In all honesty I wasn't sure it would work either. But it's actually biblical. In Philippians 4:8, Paul said to "fix your thoughts on what is true, and honorable, and right, and pure, and lovely, and admirable. Think about things that are excellent and worthy of praise" (NLT). The Amplified Bible says "center your mind on them." Why did Paul give these instructions? He wrote that "*then* the God of peace will be with you" (v. 9 NLT, emphasis added).

When we let our minds focus on the flaws and shortcomings of our spouses, we forfeit our own peace. So I made a choice. I chose to practice the exercise my counselor had suggested, and you know what? The challenge actually worked! As I leaned into the process, three minutes turned into five minutes, and I began wanting to show Jimmy more compassion. When I practiced thinking about what I loved about Jimmy, I subconsciously broke my cycle of resentment toward him.

Here's a life-changing truth I learned: *forgiveness is a decision, but reconciliation is a process.*

A MARITAL REBOOT

Forgiveness is a choice we must make, not a feeling we can fake.

Is there an area of your marriage where you *thought* you had forgiven your spouse but maybe there is 10 percent anger or frustration left that you did not express in the conversation? Perhaps that 10 percent has overtaken the 90 percent, leading you to fixate on your spouse's faults in a way that only repeats the cycle of unforgiveness.

You may need a marital reboot.

Now, you may not be a computer tech, but there's one maneuver with which you are undoubtedly familiar: Control + Alt + Delete.

Forgiveness is a choice we must make, not a feeling we can fake. Whether you're experiencing a malfunction due to a virus that has infiltrated the computer's operating system or your screen just got stuck, this function is the key to rebooting the system. Just as you find yourself with no other choice but to reset the computer in order for it to start working again, you need to reset your mind. By pressing Control + Alt + Delete, you are able to force the computer to turn off and reboot to its original operating state. Likewise, this puts action to our forgiveness.

Control

Let go of control. Let go of resentment. Resentment kills love in relationships. Maybe resentment has caused the virus of bitterness to be released in your marriage, and you need a reset. Could it be that unforgiveness toward a betrayal, infidelity, or any breach of trust has released a virus so painful that you have detached emotionally from your spouse as a survival mechanism? Love requires us to let go of control.

Alt

Take an alternative route. Do something different. Reframe the way you see your spouse. Maybe if we reframed it and thought of it from the perspective of "I can motivate my spouse by saying ____; I can encourage them by doing ____," that will give them the fuel they need as they work toward change. Go toward your spouse when you really want to run the other direction. Go toward the pain you may feel, because on the other side is intimacy.

Delete

It's time to press the Reset button and wipe the slate clean. Acknowledge where you are still holding resentment toward your spouse. Get out of the cycle of resentment and shame and begin to believe the best about your spouse.

We've all heard the old adage "Time heals all wounds." I disagree. I've known plenty of people who held on to bitterness until their dying day. The truth is that hurts must be processed, and emotions must be acknowledged and felt before we can be healed. There must be action behind our words.

Forgiveness is given, but trust is earned. Believe the best and encourage your spouse to keep doing the next right thing. Progress over perfection is the name of the game.

Romans 5:8 says, "God demonstrates his own love for us in this: While we were still sinners, Christ died for us." We were forgiven when we didn't deserve it. We were forgiven when our behaviors had not changed yet, and we continue to be forgiven. As nice as it would be, your spouse is not going to change overnight.

> **Forgiveness is given, but trust is earned.**

In every season commit to not judging, not condemning, and not shaming your spouse when he or she makes mistakes. Delete the files of resentment and shame. Your forgiveness can provide the fuel your spouse needs to continue to modify his or her behaviors and truly change.

THE ONLY PERFECT JOURNEY

We spend a lot of our time traveling these days. Security checks and overpriced water bottles are typical parts of our routine. We've even become proficient at guessing the weight of our suitcases so that I (Jimmy) don't have to be "that guy" publicly transferring junk from one bag to another, in the hopes of beating the luggage scale (which is a regular concern because I don't travel light!).

The thing about flying is that you rarely get a direct, hassle-free trip to your destination. Most of the time there's a connecting flight or, at the very least, a layover. Inconveniences easily lead to frustration, fatigue sets in, and you begin to question whether it was worth it.

Life comes with equally as many challenges: financial hardships, a wayward child, loss of a loved one, and so on. Such seasons can make you feel as though you're waiting on a delayed flight or maybe as if you got rerouted and it's taking much longer to reach your destination than you'd anticipated. Minor annoyances accumulate quickly, and each setback becomes costlier.

The reality is, we often blame our spouse in these seasons for the frustration. And although sometimes the mistakes we make do cause delays, that's part of life. No human has ever lived without a setback or mistake that required rerouting. No one has ever lived a perfect journey.

Except one.

Jesus was the only human who ever completed this journey of life perfectly. He never hindered anyone. Never caused anyone pain. Yet the Scriptures are clear: he forgave all.

Now, this doesn't mean life instantly became easy. Forgiveness doesn't eradicate hardships or struggle. All of us will at some point experience pain and even failure. But Hebrews 4:15–16 offers us this promise: "Jesus is not some high priest who has no sympathy for our weaknesses *and flaws*. . . . But He emerged victorious, without failing God. So let us step boldly to the throne of grace, where we can find mercy and grace to help when we need it most" (THE VOICE).

Jesus didn't fail, but he was tempted. He never gave in, but he understands our weaknesses.

The reason it's so important to grasp this is because the love God demonstrates goes far beyond what we deserve. It's a choice. The only One who never failed chose to forgive those who had all failed. There's no earning this kind of love—we fell short the moment we first messed up. No matter how light our baggage, we all have junk that tipped the scale. Jesus didn't.

Too often we forget this, which is exactly what the Enemy wants.

The Bible tells us that the Enemy of our souls is the devil. You may not believe it, but his primary goal is to divide, to separate. And he makes marriages one of his main targets. The reason marriages are such a sore spot for him is because marriages showcase the kind of love God has for creation. Forgiveness and reconciliation are a perfect picture of God's redemption, of two becoming one.

THE OLDEST STORY EVER TOLD

We call it two equals one, but, at the end of the day, the equation for marriage is a story. It's the oldest story ever told. God created man and then he created a "perfectly suited partner" because it wasn't good for Adam to be alone.

But the two messed up. You see, God set up Paradise with boundaries. Adam and Eve could be perfectly free—free from any form of shame, naked and fully enjoying one another . . . as long as they respected the boundaries.

Adam and Eve didn't. They violated the boundaries, and because they messed up, things became complicated. Sin entered the picture and suddenly there was distance between them and their Creator.

Now, you might think that after enough of mankind's disobeying and rejecting God, he would walk away, right? Instead, God does the unthinkable.

He forgives.

Not once, not twice, not even a hundred times, but to the point that he visited his creation in the flesh. God took on the very shame he despised—the shame that was our fault alone. In fact, he took on the burden of our sin and mistakes to the point of death.

And, in doing so, God broke the cycle.

That distance, that shame, that cycle of resentment, can be broken only by the power of forgiveness. Colossians 1:22 says that "yet Christ has now reconciled you" (AMP). His forgiveness reconciles us. This is the equation, the answer for two becoming one. It might seem impossible, even illogical, but two become one when they embrace forgiveness.

Ephesians 2:14 says, "For he himself is our peace, who has made us both one and has broken down in his flesh the dividing wall of hostility" (ESV).

This is the story of forgiveness. The story of two equals one. God demonstrates what true unity requires, and it's not compatibility. It's not that two people "complete" each other. It's not about perfection; it's about progress. It's about two broken, imperfect people, full of flaws and failures, who choose to forgive one another, who reconcile one another by choosing to forgive. Just as love has the power to turn pain into a gift, forgiveness has the power to reconcile what otherwise would have remained lost.

This is what the Enemy is afraid of because this kind of love transcends the earthly realm. It ripples into eternity. Forgiveness isn't just about longevity; it's about legacy.

A love full of forgiveness lasts forever.

A marriage made one: one of *love*, *laughter*, and *longevity*.

TWO-EQUALS-ONE CHALLENGE

There's one last challenge we want to offer you. It's something we do at every Two Equals One conference and retreat.

For this challenge you will need a Ring Pop. Yes, we mean the giant candy ring that you used to covet as a kid!

Now take a deep breath and, looking your spouse in the eyes, repeat these vows:

> I vow to allow differences not to divide us but to complete us.
>
> I vow to make our marriage my first priority.
>
> I vow to forgive fast and focus on the future.
>
> I vow to live beyond myself, love beyond my preferences, and laugh beyond my struggles.
>
> I vow not to allow working for God to replace spending time with God.
>
> I vow to have a love that has the capacity to hold your humanity.
>
> With this ring, I will savor the sweetness of our marriage.
>
> I will love you always and forever.

ADDITIONAL RESOURCES

J immy and I are here to help! This is what we do. We offer individualized coaching, couples Soulscapes, and marriage seminars. Contact us at www.twoequalsone.com.

Suicide Help

- Suicide Hotline: 1-800-273-8255

Domestic Violence Help

- National Domestic Violence Helpline: 1-800-799-7233

Substance Abuse and Mental Health Recovery

- Al-Anon: www.al-anon.org
- Celebrate Recovery: www.celebraterecovery.com
- Certified Sex Addiction Therapist: www.iitap.com
- Co-Dependents Anonymous: www.coda.org
- Covenant Eyes: www.covenanteyes.com
- Gentle Path: www.themeadows.com/about/locations/gentlepath/
- Rio Retreat Center: www.rioretreatcenter.com

- Honey Lake Clinic: www.honeylake.clinic
- Life Healing Center: www.sierratucson.com
- Recovery Ranch: www.recoveryranch.com/mental-health -treatment-programs-nashville-tn/process-addiction-treatment -center/sex-addiction-treatment-center
- Sex Addiction Intensives: www.drdougweiss.com/intensives /addiction-intensive
- Substance Abuse and Mental Health Services Administration: www.samhsa.gov

Personality Profiles

- DiSC Profile: www.discprofile.com
- Enneagram Personality Test: www.enneagramtest.com
- Love Language Quiz: www.5lovelanguages.com

Counseling/Coaching

- A Place of HOPE Counseling Center: www.aplaceofhope.com
- Crossroads Counseling of the Rockies: www.crossroadscounseling .net
- Heart to Heart Counseling: www.drdougweiss.com/addiction -intensive
- Imago Relationship Therapists: www.imagorelationshipswork .com
- Onsite: www.experienceonsite.com
- Marriage 180 Intensive: www.relationship180.com/intensives
- The Meadows Treatment Center: www.themeadows.com

ACKNOWLEDGMENTS

DR. CAROL ROBBINS–ANNAPOLIS ADHD CENTER

God knows we were a hot mess when we first came to your practice! You had two ADHD people struggling and emotionally spiraling. Two hurting people stuck in denial, abusing alcohol and food to medicate our pain. Two people in crisis, lacking communication skills with boundary and family-of-origin issues who were completely self-destructing. Our marriage was in trouble, and we couldn't see a way out of the mess we created. You gave us hope that we could and would be better if we were willing to do the work! We appreciate your honesty and tact as you patiently guided us into the dialogue that gave us the problem-solving skills to see one another, heal one another, and ultimately save our marriage. We would not be where we are without your intervention in our lives. Thank you for sticking with us and compelling us to push through hard conversations. You taught us how to navigate our brain differences with ADHD and recognize their effect on marriage. It was not only transformational for us as individuals, but together we have found it to be our superpower! Thank you for teaching us to own our part in the dysfunction and to work to change the only thing in our control, which is us. We have embraced the concept that "our spouse is our blueprint for growth." All the hard work has paid off, and now we get to help others heal. We are eternally grateful for you!

DR. WILL FRANZ—CROSSROADS COUNSELING OF THE ROCKIES

Who knew that we would finally get it and grow up? You helped us develop individually and as a couple. Your counsel and guidance helped us reach back to the little Jimmy and little Irene from childhood and care for them, heal them so they could mature to be securely attached adults. You taught us to invite the Holy Spirit into our wounds and trauma. We will never forget the holy moments that happened in your office when you had us close our eyes, pray, and ask God to "wash our imaginations." Wow! To see each other after our wounds gave us the empathy and compassion we both longed for to create safety and promote oneness in our marriage. Thank you from the bottom of our hearts.

TODD AND JULIE MULLINS—SENIOR PASTORS OF CHRIST FELLOWSHIP CHURCH, WEST PALM BEACH

There aren't enough words in the English vocabulary to express our gratitude for the open door we needed to launch the Two Equals One marriage ministry. Thank you for believing in us and what God has called us to. We can't believe we *get to* do this! May you be richly blessed for all you have sown into our lives and ministry. Thank you for being our promise pushers. We love you!

DINO AND DELYNN RIZZO

Thank you for guiding and leading us when we couldn't lead ourselves. Your time, encouragement, wisdom, and investment in us have been critical in our marriage journey. We are committed to spending the rest of our lives doing the same for others. We love you beyond measure. Fam for life!

JAMES AND VARLE ROLLINS

Thank you, Mom and Dad, for your unwavering support over the years. Thank you for the prayers and downright intercession it took to get us through the toughest times in our marriage. But God! Thank you for leaning in when we needed you and for the times you gave us the space we needed to work things out as a couple. Our family is blessed because of you both, and we love you dearly.

KEVYN AND LORI DODSON

Talk about people who stick with you through the ups and downs of life! You both have been there with us through the thick and thin, sick and sin. You are *true* friends and a gift to our lives. Thank you for listening, praying, and holding us accountable when we were stubborn and for saying the hard things when we needed to hear them. You have been our *safe couple*. Our laughs have been gut-wrenching and have brought so much healing and joy to our lives. To top it all off, you helped us stand up the dream of Two Equals One. For all the hard work, both seen and unseen, we are forever grateful.

Many lives are being affected because of your generosity with your time, talent, and treasure. We don't take lightly the sacrifices you made to help us do what we were created to do! We love you guys. Friends for life!

NOTES

Chapter 1: God's Equation for Marriage

1. Irene Rollins, *Reframe Your Shame: Experience Freedom from What Holds You Back* (Nashville: W Publishing, 2022).

Chapter 3: Turning Secrets into Strengths

1. We recommend a program like Celebrate Recovery, www.celebraterecovery.com.

Chapter 4: Complementing, Not Completing

1. Murat Ucak, "Shrapnel Injuries on Regions of Head and Neck in Syrian War," *Journal of Craniofacial Surgery* 31, no. 5 (2020): 1191–95, https://doi.org/10.1097/SCS.0000000000006345.
2. Sam Huisache, "2023 Data: 1 in 4 Americans Think Marriage Is an Outdated Concept," Clever, updated June 27, 2023, https://listwithclever.com/research/marriage-decline-survey-2023/.

Chapter 5: Redefining Love

1. *Encyclopedia Britannica*, "Leaning Tower of Pisa," accessed October 17, 2023, www.britannica.com/topic/Leaning-Tower-of-Pisa.
2. Adrian Gostick, "Harvard Research Reveals the #1 Key to Living Longer and Happier," *Forbes*, August 15, 2023, www.forbes.com/sites/adriangostick/2023/08/15/harvard-research-reveals-the-1-key-to-living-longer-and-happier/?sh=1270eaa5cf71.
3. *Merriam-Webster*, s.v. "counterpart," accessed April 7, 2024, www.merriam-webster.com/dictionary/counterpart.

Chapter 6: Cracking the Communication Code

1. Christy Bieber and Adam Ramirez, "Revealing Divorce Statistics in 2023," *Forbes*, August 8, 2023, https://www.forbes.com/advisor/legal/divorce/divorce-statistics/.
2. Chester Nez, *Code Talker: The First and Only Memoir by One of the Original Navajo Code Talkers of WWII* (New York: Penguin, 2011).
3. Bieber and Ramirez, "Divorce Statistics."

Chapter 7: The Tale of the Tiger and the Turtle

1. Jeff Thompson, "Is Nonverbal Communication a Numbers Game?," *Psychology Today*, September 30, 2011, www.psychologytoday.com/us/blog/beyond-words/201109/is-nonverbal-communication-a-numbers-game?eml.

Chapter 8: I'm in My Feelings

1. Roger R. Hock, *Forty Studies That Changed Psychology: Explorations into the History of Psychological Research*, 5th ed. (Upper Saddle River, NJ: Pearson Prentice Hall, 2005), 213–18.

Chapter 10: Check-Ins

1. A. S. L. Knol et al., "Reformulating and Mirroring in Psychotherapy: A Conversation Analytic Perspective," *Frontiers in Psychology* 11 (March 2020): 318, https://doi.org/10.3389/fpsyg.2020.00318.
2. Michael Schreiner, "Mirroring," Evolution Counseling, May 6, 2014, https://evolutioncounseling.com/mirroring/.

Chapter 11: Two Truths and a Lie

1. Lipstick pistol, 1965, USSR (KGB), Covert Action Gallery, International Spy Museum, Washington, DC, accessed April 3, 2024, www.spymuseum.org/exhibition-experiences/about-the-collection/collection-highlights/lipstick-pistol/.
2. *Oxford English Dictionary*, 2nd ed. (1989), s.v. "lie."

Part 3: Longevity

1. "Churches in Cappadocia: The Best 10 Churches You Must Visit," Cappadocia Travel Pass, April 7, 2023, https://cappadociatravelpass.com/churches-in-cappadocia-the-best-10-churches-you-must-visit; Ruwa Shah and Ahmer Khan, "In Pictures: Meet the Muslim Caretakers of Turkey's Christian Cave Churches," *Christian Science Monitor*, March 18,

2021, www.csmonitor.com/The-Culture/2021/0318/In-Pictures-Meet
-the-Muslim-caretakers-of-Turkey-s-Christian-cave-churches.

2. Max Rosenberg, "See How Turkey's Ancient Cave Dwellings Were
Transformed into a 5-Star Hotel," Business Insider India, March 14,
2013, www.businessinsider.in/See-How-Turkeys-Ancient-Cave-Dwellings
-Were-Transformed-Into-A-5-Star-Hotel/articleshow/21031669.cms.

Chapter 12: Safe Place

1. Stan Tatkin, *Wired for Love: How Understanding Your Partner's Brain
and Attachment Style Can Help You Defuse Conflict and Build a Secure
Relationship* (Oakland, CA: New Harbinger, 2011).

Chapter 13: Extreme Ownership

1. "Fast Facts: Preventing Child Abuse & Neglect," National Center for
Disease Control and Prevention, April 6, 2022, www.cdc.gov
/violenceprevention/childabuseandneglect/fastfact.html.
2. "Statistics: Children & Divorce," Owenby Law, October 11, 2018,
www.owenbylaw.com/blog/2018/october/statistics-children-divorce/.
3. "National Single Parent Day: March 21, 2023," United States Census
Bureau, March 21, 2023.

Chapter 14: #SAMETEAM

1. Edith Eva Eger, *The Choice: Embrace the Possible* (New York: Scribner,
2017), 237.
2. Eger, *The Choice*, 239.

Chapter 16: Joint Compound

1. *Oxford English Dictionary*, 2nd ed. (1989), s.v. "earnest."

Chapter 17: Boundaries

1. Tori Peglar, "How Many People Fall to Death in the Grand Canyon?,"
Outside, National Park Trips, updated February 8, 2023, www
.mygrandcanyonpark.com/park/faqs/falling-to-death-grand-canyon/.
2. Lois Tverberg, "Levav—Heart, Mind," En-Gedi Resource Center,
July 1, 2015, https://engediresourcecenter.com/2015/07/01/levav-heart
-mind; *The New Strong's Exhaustive Concordance of the Bible* (1984),
s.v. H3820, "leb."

ABOUT THE AUTHORS

Jimmy and Irene Rollins are passionate about ministry, but even more so they are passionate about marriage and the family unit. Two Equals One is all about bringing these two passions together! The mission is simple: build healthy marriages that result in healthy families, having an impact on our communities for the better.

After almost twenty-five years of full-time ministry, ten of which they served as senior pastors of i5 City, a thriving church with over three thousand members, Jimmy and Irene felt a shift in their ministry focus. They transitioned from their roles as senior pastors and yielded to the call on their lives—a call to help others build healthy marriages and families filled with *love*, *laughter*, and *longevity*.

Throughout their own marriage, Jimmy and Irene have navigated many difficulties, including food and alcohol addictions, family dysfunction, and communication issues, as well as many painful seasons of loss. For the first fifteen years of marriage, Jimmy and Irene were, as they say, "surviving but not thriving." They did their best to manage the many challenges of family life while simultaneously navigating the complexities and nuances of their professional and ministry life.

It all came to a screeching halt in 2015, when the demands of their public professional ministry life and private family and marriage life became too much for two broken individuals to manage. It was time to get help and pursue the healing they desperately needed.

Now living their best life, Jimmy and Irene are sought after globally as dynamic public speakers, authors, and marriage coaches. Offering marriage intensives for both church and corporate settings as well as individualized coaching and marriage retreats, Two Equals One is all about sharing from their wealth of experience and wisdom to inspire individuals and couples with a unique message of hope, healing, and restoration.

Jimmy is a nationally recognized speaker, marriage coach, and author who inspires diverse audiences to live beyond themselves on the journey to discovering their greater purpose. As a key strategic partner for several influential churches and parachurch organizations, Jimmy's ministry experience has been critical to architecting strategies to increase influence and realize greater impact.

Irene Rollins is a certified emotional intelligence coach and recovery activist. As a marriage educator, she loves to study human behavior and guide people to be the best version of themselves through her teaching, writing, and coaching. Irene's passion to help others overcome their self-defeating habits comes from her life experience as an overcomer of alcohol addiction and trauma.

In their downtime Jimmy and Irene enjoy reading, golfing, exercising, cooking, and clowning around with their adult children, Kayla, Jaden, and Maya, and their two English bulldog babies.

LOVE,
JIMMY & IRENE

JOIN THE TWO=ONE
COACHING COMMUNITY!

NOW THAT YOU'VE READ THE BOOK,
ARE YOU READY TO TAKE YOUR MARRIAGE
TO THE NEXT LEVEL?

JOIN THE COMMUNITY!

YOUR MARRIAGE
DOESN'T HAVE TO SUCK!

TWOEQUALSONE.COM